# So you really want to learn

# Latin
## Prep

## Book 3
## Answer Book

**Theo Zinn M.A. (Oxon.)**

**Series Editor: Nicholas Oulton M.A. (Oxon.)**

**GALORE PARK**

**www.galorepark.co.uk**

Published by Galore Park Publishing Ltd
19/21 Sayers Lane, Tenterden, Kent TN30 6BW
www.galorepark.co.uk

Printed by Charlesworth Press, Wakefield

ISBN: 978 1 902984 43 8

First printed 2006, reprinted 2007, 2011

Details of other Galore Park publications are available at
www.galorepark.co.uk

ISEB Revision Guides, publications and examination papers may also
be obtained from Galore Park.

# Acknowledgements

I am grateful as ever to Peter and Jackie and to Rupert Fennymore. Without their constant support in every way I could never have completed the six books that make up this work.

I owe a tremendous amount too to Peter Brown of Trinity College, Oxford for never failing to give of his best to every problem I have placed before him; and I thank Nicholas Oulton for having launched this whole enterprise and, after launching it, for having participated in it right from the start in a totally beneficial way.

I should also like to thank Miranda Prynne for her early work on the typesetting of this volume, and all others who have been in any way involved in this work.

And finally I am extremely thankful to all those whose kind comments have reached my ears.

# Preface

Forgive me if I begin with a few words about quantities. I was brought up very strictly on quantitites from very early days. After all, we left our prep schools trying with great enjoyment to turn English nursery rhymes into elegiac couplets. The same strictness continued at my public school, and I remember only too well the doleful tone with which the words, 'False quantity!' were uttered by our Classical Sixth form master, when we were reading aloud the passage we were about to translate.

Let me put before you, if you do not know it already, a wonderful hexameter, coming almost certainly from my prep school days; it goes:

> rēge regente ducem dūcēbant sēde sedentem.
> While the king was ruling, they were leading the general sitting on a seat.

What better way could there be of learning the different quantities in dux and dūcō, rēx and regō, sēdēs and sedeō?

Much later, at Westminster, we added a pentameter to this line; it goes:

> lēge legunt; decorant. vōce 'decōre' vocant.
> They select (him) by law; they decorate him. They call out with voice, 'O decorous one!'

Alas! I still remember most vividly discovering with horror in the night after my Latin verse paper for Honour Mods. that the 'or' of the verb decorō is short.

I must admit that I consider that studying passages by, for example, Virgil, Catullus or Horace with no concern for the metre or the quantities robs the passages themselves of most of their beauty, and the student of most of the joy of studying them. Is it, after all, so very different from studying a Beethoven sonata without any care for the blackness or whiteness of the notes or whether they have tails attached to them or not?

Finally, I hope that my books will give encouragement to all those teachers who wish their pupils to retain in after years the grammar and syntax they have learnt when they were young. Incidentally, I have never understood, and certainly do not do so now, why a pupil's prep school is not mentioned when his various places of education are enumerated in later life. I consider a 'good' prep school to be of paramount importance.

TLZ

# Chapter 1

## Exercise 1.3

1. The man who is tired desires sleep.
2. This work, which you have written, is very beautiful.
3. The place, in which we are walking, is sacred.
4. The guard, to whom I gave the sword, is sleeping.
5. You see the city which all (men) praise.
6. Many (men) gave gifts to the woman whose daughter is beautiful.
7. I do not like the boy, whom the master punished.
8. Give this gift to the girl who has read many books.
9. Have you seen the young man whose father lives in that town?
10. I praised the woman to whom I gave money.

## Exercise 1.4

1. opus, quod difficile est, nōn amō.
2. in oppidō, quod omnēs amant, habitant.
3. num est gēns quae clārior est quam nostra / clārior est nostrā?
4. Sulpicia fēmina est quam omnēs laudant.
5. custōdem, cui cibum dederāmus, spectābāmus.
6. ubi est puer, cuius sorōrem herī vīdimus?
7. dominum, quī multum vīnum bibit, servī nōn amant.
8. senem, quem cīvēs timēbant, vīdī.
9. dux, cuius cōpiae in urbe adsunt, mox discēdet.
10. nauta, cui cibum vīnumque dedimus, dormit.

## Exercise 1.5

| 1. | laudor | 3. | dēleor | 5. | aedificor | 7. | videor |
| | laudāris | | dēlēris | | aedificāris | | vidēris |
| | laudātur | | dēlētur | | aedificātur | | vidētur |
| | laudāmur | | dēlēmur | | aedificāmur | | vidēmur |
| | laudāminī | | dēlēminī | | aedificāminī | | vidēminī |
| | laudantur | | dēlentur | | aedificantur | | videntur |
| 2. | vocor | 4. | teneor | 6. | necor | 8. | terreor |
| | vocāris | | tenēris | | necāris | | terrēris |
| | vocātur | | tenētur | | necātur | | terrētur |
| | vocāmur | | tenēmur | | necāmur | | terrēmur |
| | vocāminī | | tenēminī | | necāminī | | terrēminī |
| | vocantur | | tenentur | | necantur | | terrentur |

# Exercise 1.6

1.  We are praised by the teacher.
2.  You are warned by the king, aren't you?
3.  You are being saved by your friend.
4.  You are being set free by your master.
5.  The citizens are being frightened by the soldiers.
6.  Swords are held by the enemy.
7.  I am being wounded by spears.
8.  Are you being wounded by the arrows?
9.  The boys and girls are praised by the teacher, aren't they?
10. Hurry, maid-servants! We are being called by the queen.

# Exercise 1.7

1.  gladiī ā vōbīs tenentur.
2.  hastīs vulnerāminī.
3.  ā magistrīs laudor.
4.  ā parentibus monēris.
5.  ā dominīs nostrīs līberāmur.
6.  num saevīs ventīs terrēminī?
7.  hae urbēs ā servīs occupantur.
8.  multa dōna nōbīs dantur.
9.  haec urbs mūrō servātur.
10. ā sene spectāmur.

# Exercise 1.8

1.  The wretched farmers are terrified by the cruel sailors.
2.  A big wall is being built by the inhabitants.
3.  That town is being attacked by the enemy.
4.  A great work is being prepared by Quintus, the poet.
5.  What is being carried by the boy, who is standing in the street?
6.  This maid-servant, whom you see, is often called by the queen.
7.  The gold is being moved into the temple by the slaves.
8.  The boy, whose sister is praised by all, is always being warned by the teacher.
9.  The girl, to whom a beautiful gift is being given by her mother, is very happy.
10. The wind, by which this wall is being destroyed, is savage.

# Exercise 1.9

1.  cūr gladius ab hōc puerō tenētur?
2.  oppidum ab hostibus occupātur.
3.  puella, quam parentēs amant, ā magistrīs laudātur.
4.  multī cīvēs hastīs et gladiīs vulnerantur.
5.  agricola, quī in hōc agrō labōrābat, ab amīcō salūtātur.
6.  hic servus, cuius virtūs nōta est, ā dominō līberātur.
7.  īnsula, in quā habitābāmus, marī dēlētur.

8.     puella, quācum ambulābat, ā sorōre suā spectātur.
9.     urbs, quam amābāmus, ā multīs nautīs oppugnātur.
10.    mūrus, quem vidētis, ab hīs puerīs aedificātur.

# Exercise 1.10

1.     (a) Aeneas was the son of Venus; he was a Trojan hero.
       (b) Ten years.
       (c) A wooden horse.
       (d) A man called Sinon.
       (e) They led him to King Priam.
       (f) The King of Troy.
       (g) He said that they had killed his friend and wished to kill him.
       (h) 'What does this horse, which the Greeks have left on the sea-shore, signify?'
       (i) Violate it.
       (j) Lead it safe into the city.

2.     Aeneas, the son of Venus, was a Trojan hero, who defended his city in vain. The Greeks were attacking it for ten years; but at last they departed. However, they left a wooden horse, which was very big; they also left a man called Sinon, whom the Trojans captured and led to King Priam. Then Sinon said these words: 'I am a Greek who was hateful to the Greeks; they had killed my friend and wanted to kill me; however I escaped from them.' King Priam asked Sinon: 'What does this horse, which the Greeks have left on the sea-shore, signify?' Sinon replied: 'If you violate it, you will be very wretched; therefore lead it safe into your city; for thus you will be very fortunate.'

3.     (a) urbem
       (b) Accusative plural; it is governed by per (+ acc.)
       (c) Nominative singular; it is the subject of erat (line 5).
       (d) It means 'also', and regularly comes after the noun to which it refers.
       (e) Accusative singular; direct object of cēpērunt (line 5).
       (f) It is in apposition to it.
       (g) Pluperfect.
       (h) effugiam
       (i) It is masculine singular, relating to the antecedent equus, and accusative, because it is the direct object of relīquērunt (line 12).
       (j) fēlīcior, fēlīcior, fēlīcius.

# Exercise 1.11

1.     The soldiers, whom you see, are attacking the city.
2.     We praise the farmers who are working in the field.
3.     The boys, with whom I walked into the town, are tired.
4.     The girls, whose mothers are present, are happy.
5.     The slaves, to whom the master gives nothing, are very wretched.
6.     All (men) praise the farmers by whom this wall is being built.
7.     The cities, in which many citizens live, are great.
8.     The inhabitants, whom I greatly praise, are good and wise.
9.     The walls, by which we are saved, are high.
10.    Fathers, whose sons work well, are happy.

## Exercise 1.12

1.  hī puerī cīvis, quī fortissimus est, fīliī sunt.
2.  puellae, quae in templō cantant, optimae sunt.
3.  nōlī/nōlīte mīlitēs, ā quibus incolae vulnerantur, laudāre.
4.  saevōs ventōs, quibus mūrī nostrī dēlentur, timēmus.
5.  bella quae longa sunt, pessima sunt.
6.  nōnne puellae quās vidēmus, Aulī sorōrēs sunt?
7.  gladiī, quōs tenētis, mīlitum sunt.
8.  via, quae prope templum est, nova est.
9.  servī, quibus dominī pecūniam dant, laetī sunt.
10. iter, quod fēcimus, difficile erat.

## Exercise 1.13

| 1. | mittor | 3. | pūnior | 5. | invenior |
|----|--------|----|--------|----|----------|
|    | mitteris |  | pūnīris |  | invenīris |
|    | mittitur |  | pūnītur |  | invenītur |
|    | mittimur |  | pūnīmur |  | invenīmur |
|    | mittiminī |  | pūnīminī |  | invenīminī |
|    | mittuntur |  | pūniuntur |  | inveniuntur |

| 2. | scrībor | 4. | pōnor | 6. | dēfendor |
|----|---------|----|-------|----|----------|
|    | scrīberis |  | pōneris |  | dēfenderis |
|    | scrībitur |  | pōnitur |  | dēfenditur |
|    | scrībimur |  | pōnimur |  | dēfendimur |
|    | scrībiminī |  | pōniminī |  | dēfendiminī |
|    | scrībuntur |  | pōnuntur |  | dēfenduntur |

## Exercise 1.14

1.  This city is being defended by the brave citizens.
2.  Much wine is being drunk by the soldiers.
3.  The inhabitants are being led into the city.
4.  Are we really being conquered by the enemy?
5.  You are being ruled by a good and wise king.
6.  The cities are defended by walls.
7.  Are you really being punished by the teacher?
8.  Are you not being sent into the city by the leader?
9.  I am being led into the fields by the farmers.
10. Many men are being killed in the battle with swords.

## Exercise 1.15

1.  servī in oppidum redūcuntur.
2.  mīlitēs hastīs occīduntur.
3.  pulchra dōna ab hīs mulieribus leguntur.

4.     multī librī ab hōc poētā scrībuntur.
5.     magna urbs magnīs mūrīs dēfenditur.
6.     quid ab illīs parvīs puerīs cōnsūmitur?
7.     aurum in agrō invenītur.
8.     ā sapientī rēgīnā regimur.
9.     num ā iuvenibus dūciminī?
10.    cūr ā magistrō pūnīris?

## Exercise 1.16

| 1. | ipsam | 3. | ipsīus | 5. | ipsa | 7. | ipsum | 9. | ipse |
|----|-------|----|--------|----|------|----|-------|----|------|
| 2. | ipsum | 4. | ipsum | 6. | ipsīs | 8. | ipsa | 10. | ipse |

## Exercise 1.17

1.     He himself seems to want food.
2.     The woman herself is holding a sword.
3.     I myself shall go into the town.
4.     Give this gift to the girl herself.
5.     These boys are the sons of the king himself.
6.     She herself will come.
7.     The war itself is very long.
8.     We have seen the queen herself.
9.     This slave is being called by the master himself.
10.    The leader himself is loved by the citizens.

## Exercise 1.18

1.     mūrus ipse urbem dēfendēbat.
2.     ā mīlite ipsō vulnerantur.
3.     rēgīnae ipsī pulchrum dōnum dedī.
4.     rēx ipse illōs incolās reget.
5.     ancillae ā rēgīnā ipsā vocantur.
6.     haec dōna ipsī puerō date.
7.     fīliae mulieris ipsīus pulcherrimae sunt.
8.     ducem ipsum amāmus.
9.     ipsa hunc librum nōn lēgī.
10.    uxōrem suam ipsam vīdit.

## Exercise 1.19

1.     These cities are being captured by bad men.
2.     A beautiful gift is received by the girl.
3.     Are you not being caught sight of by the enemy?
4.     We are being captured by the savage young men.
5.     I am being thrown into the sea by the cruel citizens.

6.    'Oh gold!' said the old man; 'you are greatly desired by me.'
7.    This woman is being captured by the soldiers.
8.    Why are you being captured by these citizens?
9.    The enemy are suddenly caught sight of by us.
10.   Many arrows are being thrown at us.

## Exercise 1.20

1.    cūr haec puella capitur?
2.    ab hostibus cōnspicior.
3.    haec dōna et ā puerīs et ā puellīs cupiuntur.
4.    in flūmen illud iaciuntur.
5.    ā malīs hominibus capiminī.
6.    'ō pecūnia!' dīcit dominus; 'ā bonīs servīs acciperis.'
7.    quid ab omnibus cupitur?
8.    multae sagittae ad cīvēs iaciuntur.
9.    nōnne senex ā nōbīs cōnspicitur?
10.   cūr ā vōbīs multum aurum accipitur?

## Exercise 1.21

1.    (a) Because they thought that by bringing the horse into their city they would be very fortunate.
      (b) He had been leader of the Trojans.
      (c) No; he only seemed to be present in a dream.
      (d) The fact that he was dead.
      (e) He told him to flee.
      (f) He tells him that Greek soldiers had been hiding in the horse and were destroying the city; he says that
          Aeneas would not be able to save Troy.
      (g) He tells him not to fight with the enemy.
      (h) He tells him to take the statues of their gods.
      (i) No. cum comitibus = with companions.
      (j) No. After Hector disappeared, he rushed into battle.

2.    The Trojans led the wooden horse into the city. They were very happy and they slept. Aeneas slept and in
      his sleep Hector, who was a son of Priam and himself the leader of the Trojans, seemed to him to be present;
      but he was dead; Achilles had killed him. However, Hector seemed to say these words: 'Aeneas, son of a
      goddess; I order you to flee; for Greek soldiers were hiding in the horse and have now come out; our city is
      being destroyed by them. You will not be able to save it; therefore do not fight with the enemy, but take the
      statues of our gods and together with companions carry them over many seas; at last you will find a new
      fatherland for our gods.' Hector seemed to go away, but Aeneas rushed mad(ly) into battle.

3.    (a) dormient.

      (b) Present infinitive. To be present. dīcere (line 5) = to say; fugere (line 6) = to flee; servāre (line 9) = to save; pugnāre (line 10) = to fight; abīre (line 13) = to go away.

      (c) necātur.

      (d) Vocative singular.

      (e) Nominative plural = who.

      (f) exeō, exīre, exiī, exitum = I go out.

      (g) Second person singular. Future tense of possum = you will be able.

      (h) igitur = therefore. It is generally not used first word in a sentence or clause.

      (i) Accusative plural because it follows the preposition circum (+ acc.)

      (j) invēnerās.

# Exercise 1.22

1. Annual: annus = year.
2. Insomnia: somnus = sleep; insomnia is the inability to sleep.
3. Custody: custōs = guard; a guard keeps one in custody.
4. Hour: hōra = hour.
5. Labour: labor = work.

# Exercise 1.23

1. The wine was being drunk by the soldiers.
2. The bad boys were being punished.
3. I was being wounded by arrows.
4. You were being ruled by the cruel king.
5. You were being warned by the teacher, weren't you?
6. The gold was being captured by the sailors.
7. Were we really being conquered by the enemy?
8. What was being moved, here?
9. That town was being attacked by the enemy.
10. Arrows were being thrown into the city.

# Exercise 1.24

1. hastae in templum iaciēbantur.
2. cibus ā puerīs cōnsūmēbātur.
3. ā servīs portābāris.
4. ab optimō duce dūcēbāmur.
5. hastīs vulnerābāminī.
6. ab hostibus nōn superābāmur.
7. ā patre monēbar.
8. paucī incolae ā mīlitibus capiēbantur.
9. magna nāvis ā nautīs movēbātur.
10. puerī et puellae ā magistrō audiēbantur.

# Exercise 1.25

1. bonae ancillae pulchram rēgīnam amant.
2. fortēs ducēs fessōs mīlitēs dūcēbant.
3. malus iuvenis miserum senem gladiō vulnerābat.
4. omnēs puellae sapientem magistrum audiunt.
5. parvī puerī validōs nautās vīdērunt.
6. hostēs oppidum sagittīs oppugnābant.
7. nōbilēs cīvēs vocāvimus.
8. tū meum cibum cōnsūmpsistī.
9. vōs nostrum cibum cōnsūmpsistis.
10. ingentem librum legō.

# Chapter 2

## Exercise 2.1

1. ipsōrum
2. ipsīus
3. ipsōs
4. ipsa
5. ipsīus

6. ipsa
7. ipsī
8. ipsīs
9. ipsī
10. ipsum

## Exercise 2.2

1. monērem
   monērēs
   monēret
   monērēmus
   monērētis
   monērent

2. 
   (a) regerem
       regerēs
       regeret
       regerēmus
       regerētis
       regerent

   (c) caperem
       caperēs
       caperet
       caperēmus
       caperētis
       caperent

   (e) iacerem
       iacerēs
       iaceret
       iacerēmus
       iacerētis
       iacerent

   (g) pūnīrem
       pūnīrēs
       pūnīret
       pūnīrēmus
       pūnīrētis
       pūnīrent

   (b) audīrem
       audīrēs
       audīret
       audīrēmus
       audīrētis
       audīrent

   (d) ambulārem
       ambulārēs
       ambulāret
       ambulārēmus
       ambulārētis
       ambulārent

   (f) biberem
       biberēs
       biberet
       biberēmus
       biberētis
       biberent

   (h) rogārem
       rogārēs
       rogāret
       rogārēmus
       rogārētis
       rogārent

## Exercise 2.3

1. The farmers had run into the fields in order to free the horses.
2. I came into the city lest I be alone.
3. We went out of the city as quickly as possible in order to escape from the enemy.
4. The girls were always listening to the teacher in order that they might be wise.
5. They built walls in order to defend the town.
6. You were attacking the city with arrows in order to occupy it.
7. You read this book lest you be miserable, didn't you?
8. They sailed through the sea in order to come to the island.
9. The boys used to eat good food in order to have big, strong bodies.
10. The soldiers had immediately gone to sleep, lest they should drink much wine.

# Exercise 2.4

1.  ad flūmen, ut nāvēs vidērēmus, festīnāvimus.
2.  puerī multum cibum ut validī essent cōnsūmēbant.
3.  stetistīne prope magistrum ut eum audīrēs?
4.  hostēs urbem, ut cīvēs terrērent, oppugnābant.
5.  iuvenis ille ad montēs, ut aurum invenīret, ībat.
6.  senēs in urbe, nē in perīculō essent, manēbant.
7.  quis in agrōs, ut mūrum aedificāret, iit?
8.  ut tibi dōnum facerēmus, diū labōrābāmus.
9.  mulierēs in templō, nē pugnārent, manēbant.
10. festīnāvistisne ad agrum, ut proelium spectārētis?

# Exercise 2.5

1.  (a) Hector had ordered him not to fight but to take statues of the Trojan gods and to carry them across many seas.
    (b) Because he was unable to save the city.
    (c) Because it was his destiny to find a new fatherland for the Trojan gods.
    (d) He was old and frail.
    (e) It was near to the sea.
    (f) There were mountains nearby.
    (g) He made for the mountains.
    (h) Hector had told him that he would have to sail over many seas before finding a new fatherland for the Trojan gods.

2.  Aeneas did not do what Hector had ordered him to do, but he fought in vain for his fatherland and mad(ly) underwent terrible dangers in order to save it; he had almost died; but at last his mother herself ordered him to depart; and he himself carried his father on his back and small statues of the gods on his neck and held his son in his right hand and fled towards the sea; there on the shore he found companions, men, women, boys and girls, and with them made for the mountains and there prepared a very long journey; for he had to sail far away in order to find a new fatherland.

3.  (a) Pluperfect. iubeō, iubēre, iussī, iussum = I order.
    (b) faciet.
    (c) prō patriā = on behalf of his fatherland; in tergō = on (his) back; in collō = on (his) neck; ad mare = towards the sea; in lītore = on the shore; cum eīs = with them.
    (d) Present infinitive. discēdō, discēdere, discessī, discessum = I depart.
    (e) Genitive plural; deus, -ī, m. = god.
    (f) They are all in apposition to it.
    (g) Third person singular, imperfect subjunctive active of inveniō = I find.
    (h) Because the tense of invenīret tells us that we are in historic sequence (see page 23).

## Exercise 2.6

1. The boys departed from the fields.
2. We are all hurrying into the city.
3. Many men will sail with me from the island.
4. Savage winds came down from the sky.
5. Our friends are singing in the temple.
6. Oh girls! Why are you playing in the street?
7. The women were running to the river.
8. Oh citizens! You have stood on the wall.
9. They will walk to the town.
10. Tomorrow I shall go to the mountains.

## Exercise 2.7

1. cūr ad oppidum festīnās / festīnātis?
2. crās hī puerī in templō cantābunt.
3. equī dē monte cucurrērunt.
4. ā mūrō urbis ad agrōs ībāmus.
5. puellae ab oppidō ad mare ambulāvērunt.
6. agricolae in agrīs labōrant.
7. cūr parvī puerī in mūrō stant?
8. vēnistisne ad urbem herī?
9. crās ad templum ībit.
10. mīlitēs ab urbe mox discēdent.

## Exercise 2.8

1. puerī, quī in agrō lūdunt, mulierēs, quae in oppidō sunt, vidēre possunt.
2. puellae, quae in templō sunt, mūrōs spectant.
3. hominēs, quī in nāvibus erant, meliōra dōna quam eī, quī in terrā manēbant, accēpērunt.
4. cīvibus, quī in viā erant, nōn crēdēbant.
5. omnia verba, quae in librō sunt, amāmus.
6. servī, quī in īnsulā sunt, dominum suum amant.
7. cūr senēs, quī in urbe sunt, laudās?
8. num ā iuvenibus, quī in mūrō erant, vulnerābāminī?

## Exercise 2.9

1. I saw many soldiers departing from the city.
2. That boy looking at the sky is happy.
3. Enter this temple which stands in the field!
4. Who is guarding the citizens who are running towards the city.
5. He was standing on the wall forcing everyone who was going in to go out.
6. He said bad words to me, laughing.
7. I do not praise those inhabitants who are drinking much wine.
8. The citizens sleeping in the city were not safe.
9. We love the leader who is doing many things well.
10. The very bad men who were capturing all our gold were laughing.

## Exercise 2.10

1. senem vidēmus, cibum portantem.
2. Quīntus poēta, in hāc urbe habitat, multōs librōs scrībēns.
3. crūdēlēs mīlitēs ā nōbīs spectābantur multōs incolās vulnerantēs.
4. hostēs iuvenēs urbem nostram dēfendentēs superāre nōn potuērunt.
5. omnēs hominēs Rōmānōs timēbant bellum gerentēs.
6. cīvēs vīnum bibentēs vīdī et audīvī.
7. dominum servīs suīs cibum dantem laudāvimus.
8. per montēs multa itinera fēcī, aurum petēns.
9. cūr eum nihil facientem pūnīvistis?
10. num mīlitēs in urbe nostrā dormientēs laudās?

# Exercise 2.11

1. The leader ordered his soldiers to fight bravely in order that the citizens might be safe.
2. The master forced his slaves to work well in order that everyone might praise them.
3. The king ruled the citizens well in order that they might behave well.
4. Oh boys and girls! You worked well in order that the teacher might praise you.
5. The bad young men were shouting in order that we might not be able to sleep.
6. The soldiers behaved well in order that the citizens might be happy.
7. We wanted to have many soldiers in order that the enemy might not defeat us.
8. Did you really do these things in order that the enemy might defeat us?
9. The parents gave their sons and daughters a good teacher in order that they might be wise, didn't they?
10. The teacher used to punish the boys in order that they might not behave badly.

# Exercise 2.12

1. puerō hastam dedī ut eam mīlitī daret.
2. magister puerōs et puellās, ut bene labōrārent, laudābat.
3. mīlitēs nostrī, ut hostēs fugerent, fortiter pugnāvērunt.
4. rēx in urbe cum cīvibus, nē timērent, mānsit.
5. altum mūrum, ut urbs tūta esset, aedificāvērunt.
6. rēgīna ancillās, ut celeriter venīrent, magnā vōce vocābat.
7. dux mīlitēs, nē cīvēs interficerent, discēdere iussit.
8. agricolae equīs, ut valida corpora habērent, multum cibum dabant.
9. iuvenēs, nē hostēs mulierēs caperent, fortiter pugnābant.
10. Rōmānī sociīs suīs, ut fortiter pugnārent, auxilium mittēbant.

# Exercise 2.13

1. We were walking slowly from Baiae to Rome.
2. Many poets have written long books in Athens.
3. The Romans often used to go to Baiae.
4. Many people wanted to live in Puteoli.
5. The Greeks sailed from Greece to Troy.
6. There were many people in Carthage who wanted to destroy Rome.
7. Will you really make the long journey with me from Gades to Athens?
8. Very brave men used to live in Sparta.
9. Who will walk with me to Cumae?
10. Who will return with me from Cumae to Rome?

# Exercise 2.14

1. ōlim nōbīscum Byzantiī habitābant.
2. quis nōbīscum Corinthō Troiam redībit?
3. quis Cūmīs habitābat?
4. Spartā Athēnās iter fēcērunt.
5. multī poētae Rōmae habitābant.
6. nēmō Baiīs discēdere cupit.
7. nūntiī Gādibus Carthāginem vēnērunt.
8. Londīniī diū habitābam.
9. Gādibusne Gelam ībitis?
10. Gādibus diū manēbant.

# Exercise 2.15

1. (a) Very bad people.
   (b) They drove them away from their doors.
   (c) They were tired and wanted help.
   (d) They were in disguise.
   (e) Because they were driven away by everyone.
   (f) They came at last to a very small hut.
   (g) minimum = very small.
   (h) sōlī = alone.
   (i) aequālis = of the same age.
   (j) No. They had lived together for a very long time and, although they were very poor, they were very happy.

2. There was once in Phrygia a region in which very bad men used to live. These men, used to drive away from their doors tired strangers who were approaching them and desiring help. Once upon a time Jupiter and Mercury came to this region, concealing their divine nature, and they were driven away by everyone. They were therefore very angry; but at last they came to a very small hut. There was there neither master nor slave but only the old man Philemon and his wife Baucis, who was the same age. They had lived there together for a very long time and although they were very poor they were very happy.

3. (a) (i) hominēs malī; (ii) hominēs peiōrēs.
   (b) cupiō, cupere, cupīvī, cupītum = I want, desire.
   (c) expulērunt.
   (d) Present participle, nominative, masculine plural; concealing. Appropinquantēs = approaching; cupientēs = desiring.
   (e) Therefore; this word is not used first word in a clause or sentence.
   (f) It is its superlative, nominative, masculine plural.
   (g) advenient.
   (h) sōlīus.
   (i) Pluperfect.
   (j) A concessive clause; although they were very poor.

# Exercise 2.16

1. Creed: crēdō = I believe; a creed is something that one believes.
2. Petition: petō = I seek; a petition is a request for something that one seeks.
3. Expel: pellō = I drive; to expel is to drive out. [Also repel, compel, dispel etc.]
4. Relinquish: relinquō = I leave (trans.); to relinquish is to leave.
5. Procrastinate: crās = tomorrow; to procrastinate is to leave things until tomorrow.

# Exercise 2.17

1. malī mīlitēs fortēs cīvēs petēbant.
2. nōbilēs iuvenēs miserōs puerōs servāvērunt.
3. fēminās gladiīs dēfendimus.
4. magnī puerī corpora valida habent.
5. crūdēlēs hostēs urbem nostram sagittīs oppugnāvērunt.
6. altum templum ā nōbilibus cīvibus aedificābātur.
7. bonae puellae ā dominīs suīs laudantur.
8. quattuor scūta ab hīs mīlitibus tenentur.
9. nōnne longissimum iter, ut sorōrem tuam vidērēs, fēcistī?
10. ab amīcīs vestrīs petēbāminī.

# Chapter 3

## Exercise 3.1

| | | | |
|---|---|---|---|
| 1. | laudābor | 4. | dēlēbor |
| | laudāberis | | dēlēberis |
| | laudābitur | | dēlēbitur |
| | laudābimur | | dēlēbimur |
| | laudābiminī | | dēlēbiminī |
| | laudābuntur | | dēlēbuntur |
| | | | |
| 2. | parābor | 5. | movēbor |
| | parāberis | | movēberis |
| | parābitur | | movēbitur |
| | parābimur | | movēbimur |
| | parābiminī | | movēbiminī |
| | parābuntur | | movēbuntur |
| | | | |
| 3. | spectābor | 6. | terrēbor |
| | spectāberis | | terrēberis |
| | spectābitur | | terrēbitur |
| | spectābimur | | terrēbimur |
| | spectābiminī | | terrēbiminī |
| | spectābuntur | | terrēbuntur |

## Exercise 3.2

1. Our town will soon be attacked by the enemy.
2. Both swords and spears will be carried by the soldiers.
3. Will this wall really be destroyed by savage winds?
4. Will the young men really seem to fear the boys?
5. You (pl.) will be watched by the old men.
6. You (sing.) will be ordered to remain in the town, won't you?
7. Oh maid-servants! We shall soon be called by the queen.
8. Shall I really be held by the guards?
9. A most beautiful temple will be built here by the citizens.
10. Those books will be moved by the young men.

## Exercise 3.3

1. num hic mūrus ā puerīs et puellīs aedificābitur?
2. haec arma ā iuvenibus ex urbe in agrum movēbuntur.
3. mox ā rēge līberābiminī.
4. omnēs equī ā cīvibus vidēbuntur.
5. num ā servīs superābitur?
6. saevā tempestāte terrēberis.

7. nōnne ā dominō laudābor?
8. necābunturne ab hostibus senēs?
9. num mē timēre vidēbitur?
10. agricolae ā nautīs spectābuntur.

## Exercise 3.4

| | Singular | Singular |
|---|---|---|
| Nom. | spēs | fidēs |
| Voc. | spēs | fidēs |
| Acc. | spem | fidem |
| Gen. | speī | fideī |
| Dat. | speī | fideī |
| Abl. | spē | fidē |

## Exercise 3.5

1. hōrum
2. hāc
3. hīs
4. hās
5. huius
6. hanc
7. huius
8. hī
9. hārum
10. hanc

## Exercise 3.6

1. Courage is the best of all things.
2. The sixth day will come after the fifth day.
3. No one has faith in this man.
4. Many men seek beautiful things.
5. The inhabitants are not laughing because they do not have hope.
6. This day is sacred to the god.
7. These men have more hope than those.
8. Those men are not happy although they have much property.
9. Many men want to live in our state.
10. Days are better than nights.

## Exercise 3.7

1. in ūnō annō multī diēs sunt.
2. omnēs servī bonō dominō fidem habent.
3. hī puerī multās rēs amant.
4. terrēbiminīne hīs rēbus?
5. ducibus nostrīs fidem nōn habeō.
6. is, quī numquam spē movētur, trīstissimus est.
7. rēgīna rēs pulcherrimās collēgit.
8. vēnit sacra diēs.
9. quis rem multam habēre nōn cupit?
10. rēs pūblica nostra vestrā melior est / melior est quam vestra.

# Exercise 3.8

1. dūcar
   dūcēris
   dūcētur
   dūcēmur
   dūcēminī
   dūcentur

2. mittar
   mittēris
   mittētur
   mittēmur
   mittēminī
   mittentur

3. pōnar
   pōnēris
   pōnētur
   pōnēmur
   pōnēminī
   pōnentur

# Exercise 3.9

1. pūniar
   pūniēris
   pūniētur
   pūniēmur
   pūniēminī
   pūnientur

2. custōdiar
   custōdiēris
   custōdiētur
   custōdiēmur
   custōdiēminī
   custōdientur

3. iaciar
   iaciēris
   iaciētur
   iaciēmur
   iaciēminī
   iacientur

# Exercise 3.10

1. That wine will be drunk by the sailors.
2. Oh boys, you will be caught sight of by the teacher!
3. All the citizens will be defended by these walls.
4. Bad slaves will be punished by the master.
5. Shall I really be left here by my companions?
6. Soldiers will be killed by soldiers.
7. Oh poets, we / We poets will be heard by the citizens.
8. You (sing.) will be led back safe to your parents.
9. These old men will be guarded by the young men.
10. That gold will be captured by the bad men.

# Exercise 3.11

1. hic cibus ab agricolīs cōnsūmētur.
2. multī librī ab hīs puellīs legentur.
3. omnēs malī puerī ā magistrīs pūnientur.
4. urbis mūrō dēfendēminī.
5. ā mīlitibus custōdiēris.
6. sagittae in urbem iacientur.
7. in agrum currere cōgar.
8. ab hostibus cōnspiciēmur.
9. quid ab hostibus nōn capiētur?
10. mīlitēs ā ducibus suīs dūcentur.

# Exercise 3.12

1. (a) Jupiter and Mercury.
   (b) They chased it so that the strangers could eat it.
   (c) It ran to the gods seeking help.
   (d) They stopped pursuing the goose because the gods told them not to kill it.
   (e) They were told to climb a mountain with the gods.
   (f) Yes it was. They could see nothing else except water.
   (g) Their second request was that they should be allowed to die together.
   (h) Yes. They were both turned into trees at the same time.
   (i) They deserved the rewards because they were good: they had shown hospitality to the gods even though they were very poor and did not know who their guests were.

2. The gods arrived at the hut in which Philemon and Baucis lived; the latter (two) greeted them and gave them food and tried to catch the goose by which they were guarded in order that the strangers might eat it; but it was quicker than they and fled towards the gods, seeking help. Then the strangers said 'We are gods; do not kill the goose but climb that mountain with us!' From there they saw nothing around their hut except water. They wept for their dead neighbours; but suddenly their hut was turned into a magnificent temple. The gods said 'We shall do whatever you want.' 'We want to be your priests' they said 'and, just as we have lived together, even so we want to die together' and at last, after many years, suddenly Baucis saw Philemon bursting into leaf and Philemon saw Baucis bursting into leaf: they were turned into two very beautiful trees, which bloom even today. Thus rewards are given to the good.

3. (a) deus
   (b) dabant
   (c) 3rd person plural, imperfect subjunctive of cōnsūmō. It is in the imperfect subjunctive after ut, being a final clause in historic sequence.
   (d) We could have written quam eī.
   (e) It is the perfect (past) tense. We know this because the 'u' of fūgit is long. In the present tense it would be short.
   (f) 2nd person plural, imperative.
   (g) vidēbunt
   (h) ad tugurium = to the hut
   in quō = in which
   ā quō = by which
   ad deōs = to the gods
   nōbīscum = with us
   circum tugurium = around the hut
   in templum = into a temple
   post multōs annōs = after many years
   in duās pulcherrimās arborēs = into two very beautiful trees
   (i) 1st person plural, future tense active. No; faciō has no future passive.
   (j) Accusative masculine and feminine singular of the present participle active of frondeō. frondēns = bursting into leaf.

# Exercise 3.13

1. laudātus, -a, -um = praised, having been praised
2. mōtus, -a, -um = moved, having been moved
3. spectātus, -a, -um = watched, having been watched
4. pūnītus, -a, -um = punished, having been punished
5. captus, -a, -um = captured, having been captured

6.  ductus, -a, -um = led, having been led
7.  cōnsūmptus, -a, -um = eaten, having been eaten
8.  iactus, -a, -um = thrown, having been thrown
9.  vīsus, -a, -um = seen, having been seen
10. scrīptus, -a, -um = written, having been written

## Exercise 3.14

1.  The slave, freed by his master, was fortunate.
2.  We praise the book, written by the poet.
3.  These boys, having been warned by their parents, behave well.
4.  The swords which were sought by the soldiers were not in the city.
5.  The old men were afraid, having been left by their companions.
6.  I saw the girls coming safe into the city, having been guarded by the young men.
7.  I was walking with my friend through the towns which had been occupied.
8.  Having been made king by the citizens, he was very good and very brave.
9.  See this wall, which has been built by the inhabitants!
10. I do not fear those soldiers, who have been overcome by us.

## Exercise 3.15

1.  hostēs, ā Rōmānīs victī, fūgērunt.
2.  omnia verba ā poētā scrīpta amō.
3.  mūrum ab incolīs malīs dēlētum vīdimus.
4.  puerī laudātī ex templō discessērunt.
5.  tūtaene erunt parvae puellae ā comitibus relictae?
6.  quis mulierem ā malīs iuvenibus captam servābit?
7.  sagittae in urbem iactae multōs cīvēs vulnerāvērunt.
8.  senex ab hostibus cōnspectus in urbem cucurrit.
9.  legētisne librōs ā sapientibus collēctōs?
10. equī in agrōs pulsī tūtī erunt.

## Exercise 3.16

1.  On that day he departed from Rome.
2.  We remained in the city for twelve hours.
3.  Our friends will arrive within a few hours.
4.  That woman will sing for many hours.
5.  In that year, our soldiers conquered all the enemy.
6.  They have now gone out but they will return within a few days.
7.  You have occupied our city for five years.
8.  You (pl.) will depart in the sixth year, won't you?
9.  The teacher will come at the ninth hour.
10. I have lived in this town for many years.

## Exercise 3.17

1.  Rōmam octō diēbus advenient.
2.  amīcōs nostrōs quīnque diēs exspectābāmus.
3.  illō diē hostēs tandem discessērunt.
4.  urbs paucīs diēbus oppugnābitur.
5.  equī in hōc agrō decem diēs manēbant.

6. Rōmānī multās urbēs eō annō occupāvērunt.
7. opus poētae sex hōrās legēbāmus.
8. trēs diēs cibum nōn cōnsūmēbāmus.
9. quīnque annīs hostēs redībunt.
10. puerī sextā hōrā advenient.

# Exercise 3.18

| 1. Present tense | 2. Future tense | 3. Imperfect tense | 4. Perfect tense |
|---|---|---|---|
| volō | volam | volēbam | voluī |
| vīs | volēs | volēbās | voluistī |
| vult | volet | volēbat | voluit |
| volumus | volēmus | volēbāmus | voluimus |
| vultis | volētis | volēbātis | voluistis |
| volunt | volent | volēbant | voluērunt |

# Exercise 3.19

1. 'What do you want?' he asked me. 'I want gold' I replied.
2. Those men want to fight on behalf of their friends.
3. You do want me to remain here, don't you (pl.)?
4. We shall never wish to depart from this city.
5. It is good to wish to help; but it is better to help.
6. For a long time I wanted to see my parents.
7. I shall never willingly wound these old men.
8. Because he wanted to wound the enemy, the soldier threw arrows at them.
9. This boy wants to sleep for many hours.
10. We want always to live in our city.

# Exercise 3.20

1. vīsne nōbīscum multōs diēs manēre?
2. rēgem bonum et ducēs magnōs volumus.
3. iuvenēs fēminās servāre volunt.
4. dominī servōs suōs līberāre volēbant.
5. nōn bonum est hominēs vulnerāre velle.
6. vultisne nōs discēdere?
7. mox Rōmam īre volam.
8. hostēs oppidum occupāre volēbant.
9. quis hodiē in templō cantāre vult?
10. opera ab hōc poētā scrīpta legere volō.

# Exercise 3.21

1. Volition; if one does something of one's own volition, it is because one wants to do it; volō = I wish, want.
2. Nocturnal; nocturnal means relating to the night; nox, noctis, f. = night.
3. Tempest; a tempest is a large storm; tempestās = storm.
4. Labour; labour is another word for work; labor = work.

# Exercise 3.22

1. (a) They were half brothers (they shared a mother but had different fathers).
   (b) The fact that he had disinherited his brother.
   (c) Because he knew he was going to be killed by a descendant of Aeolus and so wanted to kill them all.
   (d) He spared Aeson because of their mother.
   (e) He imprisoned him in his palace.
   (f) He treated him in this way lest he escape.
   (g) She saved him from being killed by Pelias.
   (h) She sent him to be educated.
   (i) He was sacrificing to Neptune.
   (j) He would have felt scared because he had been warned to beware of a man wearing one sandal.

2. There was a city in Thessaly called Iolcus; the king of Iolcus was Pelias; he had disinherited Aeson, who ought to have been king. Pelias was the son of Neptune; Aeson was a son of Aeolus; both Pelias and Aeson were the sons of Tyro. The prophets had said to Pelias 'because you have disinherited your brother, you will be killed by a son of Aeolus.' Pelias therefore killed very many sons of Aeolus, but he spared Aeson because of their mother; however, he imprisoned him in his palace lest he should escape. There, the wife of Aeson gave birth to a son whom Pelias immediately wanted to kill; but the mother sent her son, having secretly saved him, to Chiron, in order that he should educate him. After many years the prophets again said to Pelias 'beware of a man wearing one sandal!' and afterwards, while sacrificing to Neptune, he caught sight of a young man wearing the skin of a leopard, armed with two spears, wearing one sandal.

3. (a) Pluperfect active.
   (b) Both… and…
   (c) Being a subordinate clause, it is tucked into the clause which contains the main verb.
   (d) parcet.
   (e) coniūnx.
   (f) vult.
   (g) Accusative masculine singular of the past participle passive = saved. vestītum = clothed; armātum = armed.
   (h) Nominative masculine singular of the present participle active = sacrificing. gerentem = wearing (twice).

# Exercise 3.23

1. senēs bonī puerōs fortēs monent.
2. urbem sagittīs oppugnābāmus.
3. omnem aquam bibistī.
4. novī ducēs verba Rōmāna audiunt.
5. nōbilis dominus bonum servum līberat.
6. iter quod facitis difficile est.
7. animālia omnem cibum quem nōbīs dedistī cōnsūmpsērunt.
8. omnēs puellae ab omnibus puerīs iuvābantur.
9. cīvēs laetī erant, caelum spectantēs.
10. mūrō prope mare aedificātō dēfendēbāminī.

# Chapter 4

## Exercise 4.1

1. parātus, -a, um sum
   parātus, -a, um es
   parātus, -a, um est
   parātī, -ae, -a sumus
   parātī, -ae, -a estis
   parātī, -ae, -a sunt

2. spectātus, -a, um sum
   spectātus, -a, um es
   spectātus, -a, um est
   spectātī, -ae, -a sumus
   spectātī, -ae, -a estis
   spectātī, -ae, -a sunt

3. mōtus, -a, um sum
   mōtus, -a, um es
   mōtus, -a, um est
   mōtī, -ae, -a sumus
   mōtī, -ae, -a estis
   mōtī, -ae, -a sunt

4. cōnsūmptus, -a, um sum
   cōnsūmptus, -a, um es
   cōnsūmptus, -a, um est
   cōnsūmptī, -ae, -a sumus
   cōnsūmptī, -ae, -a estis
   cōnsūmptī, -ae, -a sunt

5. vīsus, -a, um sum
   vīsus, -a, um es
   vīsus, -a, um est
   vīsī, -ae, -a sumus
   vīsī, -ae, -a estis
   vīsī, -ae, -a sunt

6. petītus, -a, um sum
   petītus, -a, um es
   petītus, -a, um est
   petītī, -ae, -a sumus
   petītī, -ae, -a estis
   petītī, -ae, -a sunt

7. pūnītus, -a, um sum
   pūnītus, -a, um es
   pūnītus, -a, um est
   pūnītī, -ae, -a sumus
   pūnītī, -ae, -a estis
   pūnītī, -ae, -a sunt

8. trāditus, -a, um sum
   trāditus, -a, um es
   trāditus, -a, um est
   trāditī, -ae, -a sumus
   trāditī, -ae, -a estis
   trāditī, -ae, -a sunt

9. iactus, -a, um sum
   iactus, -a, um es
   iactus, -a, um est
   iactī, -ae, -a sumus
   iactī, -ae, -a estis
   iactī, -ae, -a sunt

10. custōdītus, -a, um sum
    custōdītus, -a, um es
    custōdītus, -a, um est
    custōdītī, -ae, -a sumus
    custōdītī, -ae, -a estis
    custōdītī, -ae, -a sunt

## Exercise 4.2

1. Oh maid-servant, you have been called/were called by the queen.
2. These towns have been attacked/were attacked by the enemy.
3. Very good books have been written/were written by this poet.
4. The women have been saved/were saved by the young men.
5. The temple has been destroyed/was destroyed by a storm.
6. The little girl has been guarded/was guarded by her companions.
7. I have been forced/was forced to run to the mountain.
8. The soldiers have been ordered/were ordered to fight with the enemy.
9. Many towns have been defended/were defended by brave inhabitants.
10. Why have we been left/were we left here by our friends?

## Exercise 4.3

1. cibus ā comitibus nostrīs cōnsūmptus est.
2. haec urbs ā fortibus cīvibus dēfēnsa est.

3. puerī statim ā magistrō vocātī sunt.
4. animal ā malō homine vulnerātum est.
5. illī mīlitēs ab hostibus interfectī sunt.
6. hae fēminae sagittīs vulnerātae sunt.
7. num ad mare pulsī estis?
8. hic liber ā mē in multīs locīs petītus est.
9. nōnne opera poētae ab omnibus laudāta sunt?
10. coāctane es in nāve manēre?

## Exercise 4.4

1. The young men had been loved by their parents.
2. O maid-servants, you had been loved by the queen.
3. This town had once been built by young men.
4. Had we not been forced by the cruel leader to march into the river?
5. I had been ordered to make long journeys.
6. Had you really been caught sight of by the citizens?
7. Much gold had been taken by those men.
8. The bad boys had been punished by the teachers.
9. What had been done by you?
10. We had been warned by the leader.

## Exercise 4.5

1. ab amīcīs nostrīs vocātae erāmus.
2. ā magistrō pūnītī erātis.
3. equī in agrum pulsī erant.
4. num ab agricolā fugere coāctus erās?
5. nōnne multa perīcula superāre iussus eram?
6. nōnne ā senibus hae urbēs dēfēnsae erant?
7. puellae et puerī ā magistrīs laudātī* erant.
8. multae rēs ab hostibus captae erant.
9. equī in maiōrem agrum mōtī erant.
10. nōnne monitī erātis?

* Since the participle has to be masculine (because it is agreeing with boys and girls, and the masculine prevails), it is better to write puellae et puerī, so as to bring the participle close to the masculine noun, rather than the feminine one.

## Exercise 4.6

1. I have read all these books; have you not any others?
2. In our town there is not another temple.
3. Tomorrow other boys and other girls will be present here.
4. Yesterday we hurried to the sea with other companions.
5. The swords of other soldiers are in the field.
6. The other girls' things are not here.
7. Give this money to another woman.
8. The master gave a gift not to these slaves but to others.
9. That woman is queen of another island.
10. Other towns are worse than ours.

# Exercise 4.7

1. num aliī nūntiō crēdidistī?
2. iter difficile cum aliō comite fēcī.
3. hunc cibum cōnsūmpsērunt puerī; habētisne alium cibum?
4. hī equī malī sunt; aliōs volō.
5. aliī magistrī crās ad illud oppidum ībunt.
6. num ab aliīs ducibus dūcēminī?
7. mox aliud oppidum vidēbō.
8. nōnne hic iuvenis alterīus mulieris fīlius est?
9. num aliōrum poētārum opera amās?
10. ab aliā rēgīnā tum regēbantur.

# Exercise 4.8

nōlō, nōlle, nōluī = I do not wish

| Present indicative | | Imperfect indicative | |
|---|---|---|---|
| | nōlo | | nōlēbam |
| | nōn vīs | | nōlēbās |
| | nōn vult | | nōlēbat |
| | nōlumus | | nōlēbāmus |
| | nōn vultis | | nōlēbātis |
| | nōlunt | | nōlēbant |

| Future indicative | | Perfect indicative | |
|---|---|---|---|
| | nōlam | | nōluī |
| | nōlēs | | nōluistī |
| | nōlet | | nōluit |
| | nōlēmus | | nōluimus |
| | nōlētis | | nōluistis |
| | nōlent | | nōluērunt |

| Imperfect subjunctive | |
|---|---|
| | nōllem |
| | nōllēs |
| | nōllet |
| | nōllēmus |
| | nōllētis |
| | nōllent |

# Exercise 4.9

1. We do not wish to fight with the Romans.
2. Who will not wish to run to the walls with me?
3. Why do you not wish to laugh with us?
4. These slaves do not wish to work in the fields.
5. You do not wish to help the boys and the girls.
6. I refused/did not wish to go with those soldiers.
7. Oh inhabitants, do not wound the old men.
8. You often did not wish to do this.
9. It is bad not to wish to do good things.
10. Why does the boy not wish to read these books?

# Exercise 4.10

1. cūr nōlunt fēminae dē monte ad mare venīre?
2. urbem oppugnāre nōlent.
3. Mārce, nōlī multum vīnum bibere!
4. hī mīlitēs in hāc urbe manēre nōlunt.
5. cūr id quod magister tē facere iubet facere nōn vīs?
6. in agrōs cum aliīs cīvibus īre nōluit.
7. aliōs iuvenēs vulnerāre nōlumus.
8. hic parvus puer in templō sōlus cantāre nōn vult.
9. iter difficile sine amīcīs facere nōlēbat.
10. cūr ad flūmen festīnāre nōn vultis?

# Exercise 4.11

1. (a) rēx Iōlcī.
   (b) He had imprisoned him.
   (c) He was greatly terrified.
   (d) He promised to hand over his kingdom to him.
   (e) No. He built it with the help of Minerva.
   (f) He had collected some companions.
   (g) Because they sailed in the Argo.
   (h) No. There were very famous men among them, for example Hercules, Orpheus and Lynceus.
   (i) Because of his excellent eyesight.

2. Pelias asked the young man, 'Who are you?' 'I am Jason,' he replied, and he himself asked Pelias, 'And who are *you*?' Pelias replied, 'I am Pelias, King of Iolcus.' 'You are not,' said Jason, 'for Aeson, my father, imprisoned by you, ought to be king.' Pelias, greatly frightened, said, 'Sail to Colchis and from there take the fleece of a golden ram which is hanging on the branches of a tree in the forest of Mars, and give it to me: and I shall hand over your kingdom to you.' Then Argus built the ship, Argo, with the help of Minerva; and that was the first 'long ship' (i.e. battle ship); and among the companions chosen by Jason, who were called Argonauts, many were very famous. For Hercules was present and Orpheus and Lynceus, who had excellent eyes. Thus the journey was being prepared.

3. (a) respondēbit.
   (b) The word rēx is in apposition to Pelias. In line 4, Aeson, pater meus = Aeson, my father. In lines 9-10, nāvem, Argō = the ship, (called) Argo.
   (c) It is the past participle passive. territus = frightened (line 6), collēctōs = gathered together (line 12).
   (d) Ablative plural, after in (+ abl.) = in, on.
   (e) Present participle = hanging.
   (f) It refers to pellem.
   (g) Imperative (sing.) of dō, dare, dedī, datum = I give. nāvigā (line 6) = sail! cape (line 8) = take!
   (h) Ablative singular; with the help.
   (i) vocātī sunt.
   (j) The superlative. optimōs = very good.

# Exercise 4.12

1. Oh friends, we shall guard ourselves in the temple.
2. Marcus, you have been saved by yourself.
3. Oh soldiers, why do you praise yourselves?
4. I shall not hand myself over to the enemy.
5. I gave myself a beautiful gift.
6. Will you really be wounded by yourselves?
7. Do we not have faith in ourselves?
8. I forced myself to work.
9. We have set ourselves free.
10. Listen to yourselves shouting!

# Exercise 4.13

1. puellae, vōs ipsās in aquā flūminis vīdistis.
2. Sulpicia, ā tē ipsā servāta es.
3. nōbīs ipsīs multa verba dīximus.
4. iuvenēs, cūr semper vōs ipsōs laudātis?
5. mē ipsam cantantem saepe audiō.
6. nōs ipsōs gladiīs et hastīs dēfendimus.
7. tibi ipsī pulchrum dōnum dedistī.
8. hastīs nōs ipsās dēfendēmus.
9. mē ipsum numquam laudō.
10. 'vōbīs ipsīs gladiōs date!' dīxit dux.

# Exercise 4.14

1. The girls are often praised by the same master.
2. The same town was attacked again by the enemy.
3. In this year the old man gave a reward to the same young man.
4. All those men are citizens of the same town.
5. That citizen lives in the same city as I do.
6. Marcus and Aulus hurried into the city in order to meet the same wise man.
7. Both you and I love the works of the same poet.
8. This soldier fought in the same battle as that one did.
9. These young men love the same woman.
10. We all have the same teacher.

# Exercise 4.15

1. eundem puerum in templō cantantem audīvimus.
2. ego et amīcus meus ut eandem urbem iterum vidērēmus, longum iter fēcimius.
3. num eiusdem mātris fīliī sunt?
4. semper eīdem ducī crēdidī.
5. idem aurum quod amīcī vestrī petēbātis.
6. hic senex eōdem gladiō quō ille vulnerātus est.
7. nōs cīvēs omnēs ab eādem rēgīnā regimur.
8. omnēs eundem librum legere volumus.
9. hī librī omnēs eiusdem magistrī sunt.
10. illa dōna omnia eīdem fēminae dā/date.

# Exercise 4.16

1. He wandered for thirty years through lands and seas.
2. A thousand men live in this town.
3. I made a journey with seventy companions.
4. Forty horses are standing in the same field.
5. Fifty boys will read books here.
6. That city was saved by a hundred young men.
7. All the teachers praised these eighty girls.
8. Give a hundred swords to these one hundred soldiers.
9. Our leader is master of ninety slaves.
10. One hundred boys were heard by the citizens singing.

# Exercise 4.17

1. quadrāgintā et quīnquāgintā nōnāgintā sunt.
2. trīgintā et septuāgintā centum sunt.
3. sexāgintā et decem septuāgintā sunt.
4. octōgintā et vīgintī centum sunt.
5. trīgintā et vīgintī quīnquāgintā sunt.
6. quīnquāgintā et quīnquāgintā centum sunt.

# Exercise 4.18

1. in hāc terrā quadrāgintā oppida sunt.
2. septuāgintā diēs in urbe manēbāmus.
3. per agrōs cum centum comitibus festīnāvī.
4. sexāgintā puerīs librōs dedimus.
5. mīlle mīlitēs hanc urbem oppugnāvērunt.
6. hī hominēs octōgintā mulierum custōdēs sunt.
7. quīnquāgintā senēs in illō proeliō pugnābant.
8. num trīgintā equī dē monte cucurrērunt?
9. in hōc agrō nōnāgintā iuvenēs adsunt, labōrantēs.
10. in oppidō centum cīvēs vīdī.

# Exercise 4.19

1. The citizens were greatly afraid while the enemy remained in the city.
2. Sulpicia suddenly cried out, 'Do not fight!' while Marcus was fighting with Aulus.
3. While I was hurrying into the town I saw an old man, wounded.
4. All of you were very brave while the city was being attacked.
5. The sailors suddenly found water while they were seeking wine.
6. While I was watching the mountains I suddenly saw a horse.
7. The poet sings while he is writing.
8. While it was night, we were frightened by a storm.
9. While the soldier is sleeping, we are very happy.
10. While we were reading the book, the teacher suddenly departed.

# Exercise 4.20

1. dum in urbe bibō, Mārcī vōcem subitō audīvī.
2. dum puellae in templō cantābant, puerī in agrīs lūdēbant.
3. dum librum legit, magister advēnit.
4. dum māter cibum parat, Mārcus subitō rīsit.
5. dum hostēs urbem oppugnābant, Quīntus librum suum scrībēbat.
6. servī, dum dominum audiunt, labōrant.
7. dum viam spectāmus, Aulus eam trānsiit.
8. dum mīlitēs urbem dēfendēbant, cīvēs tūtī erant.
9. dum puerī gladiōs tenent, Titus vulnerātus est.
10. dum senēs ambulant, iuvenēs currunt.

# Exercise 4.21

1. (a) No. They met many dangers.
   (b) He hoped that Jason would be killed.
   (c) He promised to hand over the fleece to Jason.
   (d) She helped Jason because she had fallen in love with him.
   (e) Her help was effective thanks to her magic arts.
   (f) The serpent's teeth became soldiers.
   (g) Refused.
   (h) It never slept.
   (i) She sent it to sleep.

2. At last the Argonauts set sail and after many dangers arrived at Colchis; there King Aeetes said to Jason, 'Yoke two fire-breathing bulls and plough the field of Mars and sow there the teeth of a serpent and I shall hand over to you the fleece.' Because she had fallen in love with Jason, the daughter of the king, Medea, helped him with magic arts. With her help, he yoked the bulls, ploughed the field, and sowed the teeth. They, having been turned into soldiers, either killed or wounded each other. But Aeetes refused to hand over the fleece. This fleece was guarded by a very huge dragon which never slept. Medea sent it to sleep and the Argonauts took the fleece; and they escaped in the ship together with Medea.

3. (a) Accusative plural, after the preposition post (+ acc.).
   (b) It is in apposition to rēx.
   (c) Present participle; it means breathing.
   (d) Imperative; it means 'yoke!' arā (line 4) = plough! sere (line 4) = sow!
   (e) Future of trādō.
   (f) Pluperfect.
   (g) iuvābit.
   (h) Past participle passive, nominative masculine plural.
   (i) eī pellī.
   (j) It is its superlative.

# Exercise 4.22

1. bonus puer in magnō templō cantābat.
2. validī cīvēs fortium mīlitum auxiliō mūrum aedificant.
3. laetī iuvenēs miserōs senēs dēfendēbant.
4. rēx nōbilis clārum poētam audīvit.
5. omnia scūta movēbāmus.
6. in urbem ut cīvēs servārēmus festīnāvimus.
7. num illa urbs ab hostibus dēlēta est?
8. dum librōs nostrōs legimus, mīles interfectus est.
9. cūr magistrī puerōs laudāre nōlunt?
10. crās idem iter faciēmus.

# Chapter 5

## Exercise 5.1

1.  He always runs along the same roads.
2.  This woman was preparing the same food for the same boys.
3.  Tomorrow I shall make a journey with the same companions.
4.  These swords belong to the same soldiers.
5.  We were saying the same words as you.
6.  The teachers used to give the same gifts to the same girls.
7.  You always read the same books.
8.  We are all defended by the same walls.
9.  The same boys do the same things.
10. All the boys and girls are playing in the same fields.

## Exercise 5.2

1.  semper eōsdem equōs in eīsdem agrīs stantēs vidēmus.
2.  multae mulierēs ab eīsdem urbibus discessērunt.
3.  hī librī omnēs eārundem puellārum sunt.
4.  illī magistrī eōsdem puerōs pūnīvērunt.
5.  eadem scūta mīlitibus dabāmus.
6.  eadem itinera faciēmus quae tū/vōs.
7.  hī nautae semper in eīsdem nāvibus nāvigant.
8.  eadem hīs cīvibus date.
9.  eīdem senēs ab eīsdem mīlitibus vulnerātī sunt.
10. omnēs eōsdem ducēs laudant.

## Exercise 5.3

| Present | Future | Imperfect | Perfect |
|---|---|---|---|
| ferō | feram | ferēbam | tulī |
| fers | ferēs | ferēbās | tulistī |
| fert | feret | ferēbat | tulit |
| ferimus | ferēmus | ferēbāmus | tulimus |
| fertis | ferētis | ferēbātis | tulistis |
| ferunt | ferent | ferēbant | tulērunt |

## Exercise 5.4

1.  Soldiers, what are you carrying? We are carrying swords and spears.
2.  Why are you carrying many books? I wish to read them.
3.  Oh Marcus, bring me help.
4.  Aeneas was carrying his father out of the city.
5.  The master collected together slaves in order that they might carry gold into the temple.
6.  This very wretched old man is bearing many woes.
7.  Why do I always bear the anger of the king?
8.  Winds will soon bring a storm into our town.
9.  I do not wish to carry all these things.
10. Why are those men carrying these shields? Because you are not carrying them.

# Exercise 5.5

1.   servī īram dominī suī ferre nōn poterant.
2.   senēs in urbem aquam ferēbant.
3.   ō Sulpicia, nōnne cibum et vīnum fers?
4.   mīles ille gladium et scūtum fert.
5.   malī nautae per urbem hastās ferentēs ībant.
6.   aurum ex flūmine et ā montibus ferō.
7.   fēminae auxilium cīvibus vulnerātīs ferunt.
8.   num hic equus tē Rōmam feret?
9.   cūr laetī estis? quod in urbem nostram aurum ferimus.
10.  magna perīcula fortiter fertis.

# Exercise 5.6

1.   They were attacking the whole town with arrows.
2.   I was fighting with the enemy throughout the battle.
3.   He read the whole of these books in order to be wise.
4.   While they were singing in the temple, we were walking through the whole of the field.
5.   Are the boys playing through the whole of the road?
6.   O slaves, the master is totally angry.
7.   Do not build part of a wall, but build a whole wall.
8.   This whole place has seven parts.
9.   Savage winds move whole rivers.
10.  That city is the greatest part of our whole fatherland.

# Exercise 5.7

1.   tōtae urbēs ventīs dēlētae sunt.
2.   tōtae cōpiae hostium ā nostrīs mīlitibus victae sunt.
3.   tōtum librum quem magister nōbīs dedit lēgimus.
4.   bonī iuvenēs hunc tōtum mūrum aedificāvērunt.
5.   ille puer, quod tōtus īn somnō est, magistrum nōn audit.
6.   tōtī īnsulae novem partēs sunt.
7.   hoc tōtum iter difficillimum est.
8.   in tōtō bellō peius proelium nōn erat.
9.   haec verba tōtīus operis pars sunt ā poētā scrīptī.
10.  num per tōtum flūmen nāvigāvistis?

# Exercise 5.8

1.   (a) He was in the mountains.
     (b) He was building a fleet of many ships.
     (c) They were doing this in order to find a new fatherland.
     (d) She ordered Aeolus to destroy the Trojan fleet with winds.
     (e) Her plot was foiled because Neptune ordered the winds to stop.
     (f) Dido was in this land because she had been driven out of her fatherland.
     (g) She was building a new city.
     (h) Dido fell in love with Aeneas when she heard him tell the story of the fall of Troy.
     (i) It was so effective because he had been sent by Jupiter.
     (j) Aeneas himself did not found Rome; but Romulus and Remus, who did found Rome, were his descendants.

2. We left Aeneas with his father and son and companions in the mountains; all of them were building a fleet of many ships in order to find their new land. And finally they set sail; but the goddess Juno, who did not like the Trojans, ordered Aeolus, the god of the winds, to destroy their fleet with winds. However Neptune forced them to stop. Then the fleet, almost destroyed, came to a land in which Queen Dido, driven with companions from her fatherland, was building a new city, Carthage. With her help, Aeneas repaired his fleet and he remainded for a long time in Carthage. For when she heard the story of the fall of Troy told by him, Dido fell in love with him; but Mercury, sent by Jupiter, ordered him to depart. Finally he reached Italy. There he founded a city called Lavinium. Afterwards Ascanius his son founded Alba Longa; and the descendants of Aeneas, Romulus and Remus, founded Rome.

3. (a) Ablative plural; comes.
   (b) Perfect (past) tense of relinquō; here it means 'we left'.
   (c) It is imperfect subjunctive, because it is in a purpose clause introduced by ut.
   (d) Iūnō is in apposition to dea.
      Aeolum, ventōrum deum (lines 5-6) = Aeolus, god of the winds;
      Dīdō rēgīna (line 9) = Dido, the queen;
      novam urbem Carthāginem (line 10) = a new city, Carthage;
      urbem... nōmine Lāvīnium (lines 15-16) = a city... Lavinium by name;
      Ascanius fīlius eius (line 16) = Ascanius, his son;
      posterī... Rōmulus et Remus (lines 17-18) = descendants, Romulus and Remus.
   (e) iubēbit.
   (f) Past participle passive of dēleō. expulsa (line 9) = driven away; nārrātam (line 13) = having been told; missus (line 14) = sent.
   (g) Ablative; with her help.
   (h) It is a subordinate clause tucked in between the subject Dīdō and the main verb adamāvit.
   (i) advenīret.
   (j) It is an adverb.

# Exercise 5.9

1. The teacher advised the boys to read the book.
2. We asked the sailors to depart.
3. The masters had warned the slaves not to work badly.
4. The inhabitants often asked the king to give help to the old men.
5. The enemy warned us to remain in the city.
6. The farmer used to ask the boys not to play in the field.
7. Why did they advise you to run to the river?
8. Had they really asked you to drink much wine?

# Exercise 5.10

1. puerōs ut in agrīs lūderent monuī.
2. mīlitem nē senem vulnerāret rogāvimus.
3. dux nōs ut in urbe manērēmus monuit.
4. rogāvēruntne tē ut illōs librōs legerēs?
5. vōs nē in viā stārētis monuī.
6. eōs ut discēderent rogāvī.
7. nōs ut mare spectārēmus monēbant.
8. nōs nē prope templum clāmārēmus rogāvit.

# Exercise 5.11

1. The leader ordered the soldiers to rush upon the enemy.
2. We persuaded the boys to behave well.
3. The queen had ordered her maid-servants to prepare food.
4. I persuaded the girls not to play in the street.
5. The teachers often ordered us not to shout.
6. The farmers persuaded the inhabitants to build a wall.
7. I ordered those wicked young men not to wound the horses.
8. I persuaded the citizens to defend the city.

# Exercise 5.12

1. māter nostra nōbīs ut multōs et bonōs librōs legerēmus persuāsit.
2. rēx incolīs ut decem mūrōs aedificārent imperāvit.
3. quis vōbīs ut ab urbe discēderētis persuāsit?
4. nōnne dux iuvenibus ut in agrīs labōrārent imperāvit?
5. hostibus nē urbem nostram oppugnārent persuāsimus.
6. quis cōpiīs nostrīs ut ab īnsulā discēderent imperāvit?
7. nōnne vōbīs nē illud iterum facerētis imperāvī?
8. num senēs iuvenibus ut captōs cīvēs servārent imperāverant?

# Exercise 5.13

feror
ferris
fertur
ferimur
feriminī
feruntur

# Exercise 5.14

1. What is being carried to me?
2. We are being carried through the sea by ships.
3. They are being carried by great waves to the land.
4. Why are you being carried by the boys?
5. I rush into battle.
6. Are you really rushing into the river?
7. The wounded horse is being brought to the farmer.
8. Spears are being brought to the soldiers by young men.

# Exercise 5.15

1. cibus ad mē fertur.
2. senēs ā iuvenibus feruntur.
3. ad flūmen ferimur.
4. quid ad ducem fertur?
5. cūr ā cīvibus ferris?
6. feriminīne ad īnsulam hīs nāvibus?
7. ad templum feror.
8. mulierēs ad urbem feruntur.

# Exercise 5.16

1. (a) He was King of Clusium.
   (b) Yes; there was a wooden bridge which it was easy to cross.
   (c) They were terrified because they feared the Etruscans would cross the bridge and reach Rome.
   (d) Horatius told the Romans to destroy the bridge so that the Etruscans could not cross it.
   (e) Horatius was on the furthermost part of the bridge.
   (f) No; he was alone at first but then he had two companions, Spurius Lartius and Titus Herminius.
   (g) He turned to Father Tiber.
   (h) He asked for help.
   (i) Yes. He managed to swim safely to the Roman shore.
   (j) It was all the more remarkable in that he was wounded with many wounds.

2. Lars Porsenna, King of Clusium, an Etruscan city, was waging war with (i.e. against) the Romans. Rome was defended by walls and by the River Tiber, but there was a wooden bridge called Sublicius over which it was easy to cross the river. The Etruscans were rushing to the bridge and the Romans, terrified, were fleeing. But one man, called Horatius Cocles, ordered them to destroy the bridge so that the enemy could not cross the river. Meanwhile he himself, on the furthermost part of the bridge, was resisting very many Etruscan soldiers, at first alone, then with two companions, Spurius Lartius and Titus Herminius. However, when the bridge had already nearly been destroyed, Horatius ordered these (two) men to run across it as

quickly as possible. But he himself remained, mocking the enemy and defending himself with his shield. At last the bridge fell and Horatius begged Father Tiber to bring help to him and he jumped down into the river and, although he was wounded with many wounds, he swam safe to the Roman shore.

3.      (a) It is in apposition to it.

           urbis Etruscae is in apposition to Clūsiī (line 1) = of Clusium, an Etruscan city;

           Tiberī is in apposition to flūmine (lines 2-3) = by the river Tiber;

           Horātius Coclēs is in apposition to vir (line 6) = a man, Horatius Cocles;

           Sp. Lartiō and T. Herminiō are in apposition to comitibus (line 10) = with; companions, Spurius Lartius and Titus Herminius;

           Tiberim is in apposition to patrem = the father, Tiber.

           Sublicius (line 4) is an adjective (= supported by piles) and is not therefore in apposition to pōns (line 3).

      (b) Perfect (past) passive.

      (c) It is the present infinitive active of trānseō; trānsīre (line 7) = to cross; dēlēre (line 8) = to destroy; currere (line 13) = to run.

      (d) It is neuter.

      (e) It is a purpose clause.

      (f) sōlīus, sōlī.

      (g) It is an adverb.

      (h) They are present participles.

      (i) It is an indirect command.

      (j) adnāverat.

# Exercise 5.17

1.    volō (= I wish) + voluntary; voluntary means according to one's wishes.
2.    tōtus (= whole) + total; total means whole.
3.    somnus (= sleep) + insomnia; insomnia means an inability to sleep.
4.    paene (= nearly) + peninsula; a peninsula is almost an island.
5.    mīlle (= thousand) + millennium; a millennium is a period of a thousand years.
6.    imperō (= I command) + imperious; imperious means bossy!
7.    rīdeō (= I laugh) + deride; to deride is to laugh at.

# Exercise 5.18

1.    parvī puerī fortēs iuvenēs laudāvērunt.
2.    crūdēlis mīles miserum senem gladiō occīdit.
3.    laetī cīvēs pulchra verba audiēbant.
4.    hostēs urbem nostram multīs sagittīs oppugnābant.
5.    omnēs meōs librōs lēgistī.
6.    in urbem ut eam dēfenderēmus festīnāvimus.
7.    num mīlitēs nē flūmen trānsīrent monuistis?
8.    per agrōs ambulābat, rīdēns.
9.    labōrāre coāctī, miserī erāmus.
10.   opus, quamquam difficile est, bene faciēmus.

# Chapter 6

## Exercise 6.1

The Greeks had given to Agamemnon a girl captured from the town Chryse; her father, a priest of Apollo, brought to the Greeks very many most beautiful gifts in order to ransom his daughter. But, although the soldiers supported the priest, Agamemnon cursed him and commanded him to depart. He begged Apollo to bring him help and Apollo killed very many Greeks with disease. At last Achilles asked the prophet Calchas, 'Why is Apollo punishing us?' Calchas, terrified, answered, 'Because Agamemnon refused to give back the daughter to her father.' Agamemnon was very angry but Achilles defended the prophet. Then Agamemnon and Achilles quarrelled with each other; and finally the former said to the latter, 'I shall give back to the priest his daughter, but I shall take your girl Briseis instead of her.' Then Achilles said, 'I shall no longer enter into battle.' And with his friend Patroclus he departed; and Agamemnon took Briseis.

  (a) He was a priest of Apollo.
  (b) He came to ransom his daugher.
  (c) He brought very many most beautiful gifts.
  (d) The Greek army supported him.
  (e) No; Agamemnon did not feel the same.
  (f) The father begged Apollo to bring him help.
  (g) Achilles asked the prophet, 'Why is Apollo punishing us?'
  (h) Agamemnon was very angry because he did not wish to give up his girl.
  (i) Agamemnon threatened Achilles by saying that he would give up the girl, but would take Achilles' girl instead.
  (j) Achilles said that he would no longer go into battle.

## Exercise 6.2

Achilles begged his mother Thetis, who was a goddess, to bring him help; and she begged Jupiter to favour the Trojans. And while Achilles did not wish to fight, Hector, leader of the Trojans, the oldest of the sons of King Priam, was overcoming all the Greeks. Agamemnon was greatly upset and finally sent three leaders, Phoenix, Ajax and Ulysses, to the huts of the Myrmidons, in order to call Achilles back into battle. Phoenix, who was an old man, had educated Achilles from his boyhood and was very greatly loved by him; Ajax was the best of the Greek heroes after Achilles; Ulysses was the cleverest and the most cunning. These men tried to persuade Achilles to return to the battle. Agamemnon had promised very many most beautiful gifts; he had decided to give back Briseis. But although the Greeks were being overcome by the Trojans and especially by Hector, although they were in very great danger, although they very greatly longed for Achilles, Achilles did not return into the battle.

## Exercise 6.3

While the Greeks were being overcome, Patroclus begged Achilles to lend him his most excellent, strong arms. Because he loved him greatly, Achilles lent him his arms; and Patroclus went into battle. There he fought with Hector and was killed by him. And Hector carried off the arms of Achilles, among which was a magnificent shield. When he learnt of the death of Patroclus, Achilles grieved very greatly, and at last returned into the battle. But beforehand he begged his mother Thetis to obtain new arms for himself from the god Vulcan. And Vulcan made arms, among which was a most magnificent shield. Armed with these, Achilles fought with Hector; and he killed him; and he dragged his body around the walls of Troy. Priam, the old man, father of Hector, defended by the gods, went to the huts of the Greeks and begged Achilles to give back to him the body of his son. Achilles, mindful of his own father, gave back the body of Hecor to his father; and the Trojans prepared to bury Hector.

(a) It is the superlative of bonus.
(b) It is in the subjunctive because it comes after ut in an indirect command.
(c) It is in the accusative, because in here means into.
(d) doluērunt.
(e) 3rd person singular, perfect (past) tense active of redeō.
(f) It is in apposition to it.
(g) Accusative singular of corpus.
(h) in proelium (lines 4-5) = into the battle; cum Hectore (line 5) = with Hector; ab eō (line 5) = by him; in quibus (line 6) = in (among) which; in proelium (line 9) = into the battle; ā deō (line 10) = from the god; in quibus (line 11) = in (among) which; cum Hectore (line 13) = with Hector; circum mūrōs (line 14) = around the walls; ā dīs (line 15) = by the gods; ad māgālia (line 16) = to the huts.
(i) Past participle passive of dēfendō.
(j) patrum.

# Exercise 6.4

(i) crūdēlēs hostēs urbem magnam sagittīs oppugnābant.
(ii) fortis mīles senem perterritum gladiō dēfendit.

# Exercise 6.5

After Claudius came Nero; when he was born his father said about him, 'No one can be born from me and Agrippina who will not be hateful.' Agrippina was the mother of Nero. He, under Caligula, his uncle, had two tutors, a dancer and a barber. He was adopted by Claudius, who had married Agrippina, although he had his own son, Britannicus; and he (Nero) had as tutor Seneca. When Claudius died, he was made emperor in his seventeenth year. He praised his mother very greatly. On the first day of his rule, he gave the sentrymen as a password, 'The best of mothers.' But when she did not receive from him enough power, she favoured Britannicus. Nero killed him with poison, as men said, when he was fourteen years old. On the whole, however, he behaved kindly, and tried to please everyone. When he had to sign a death sentence, he said, 'I wish I was unable to write.' For five years he handed over nearly everything to Seneca, who carried out all affairs 'in the way of the ancestors'. He (Nero) himself enjoyed himself; and these years were called very happy.

(a) He said that no one born from him and Agrippina could fail to be hateful. He had no illusions about himself.
(b) No; he entrusted his education to a dancer and a barber.
(c) Yes; he had a son of his own.
(d) No; he was only seventeen.
(e) He greatly praised her, and gave as their first password to the sentrymen the words, 'Best of mothers'.
(f) He did not give her enough power.
(g) As a result, she transferred her favour to Britannicus.
(h) He is said to have solved the problem by poisoning him.
(i) He did not like it, saying that he wished that he could not write.
(j) No; he handed over almost everything to Seneca and merely enjoyed himself.

# Exercise 6.6

Nero's mother, Agrippina, entered into plots against her son. He began to fear her more and more; finally he decided to murder her; to the soldier who was killing her she* said, 'Strike my womb.' After his mother's murder, (Nero) was not blamed by men as he feared (he would be), but he was very greatly praised, because she was greatly hated. Because he did not love his wife Octavia, an innocent woman, whom he married when he was sixteen, he divorced her. She was finally murdered. He married Poppaea, whom he loved outstandingly; she was totally unlike Octavia, but once, when he returned home late, having been reproached by her, he kicked her in anger and she died. Nero very greatly loved the arts of the Greeks; he wished to persuade the senators to love them also; he forced highly dignified men and women to dance and to act; he himself used to write poems and persuaded others to write; he himself used to sing on the stage. He also killed many people; he took money from many people; he behaved most disgracefully and then the city of Rome was laid waste by a huge fire.

\* The Latin is rather misleading here, I fear. The subject of dīxit would appear to be he, but it was in fact Agrippina who said this.

# Exercise 6.7

The very great fire destroyed a large part of Rome. Although Nero gave the citizens every kind of help, they hated him very greatly because he built for himself a magnificent golden house where there had been small dwellings. They used to say, 'Nero destroyed the city with fire on purpose, in order to make it very beautiful.' They also spoke thus: 'While watching the flames, Nero was praising them because they were so beautiful, and he was singing a song about them written by him about the fall of Troy.' He accused the Christians of arson and punished them in a most cruel manner. Then some conspirators tried to kill Nero and to make Piso, a man who was not much better (than Nero), emperor, but they were betrayed and were themselves killed. Then Nero departed to Greece and sang there in many cities and received prizes from all; and he liberated the whole of the province of Greece from the Romans. When he returned to Rome leaders of the soldiers mutinied; having been proclaimed a (public) enemy by the senators he said, 'What an artist do I perish!' And fearing a most savage death, he killed himself with difficulty with the help of a servant.

   (a) Nominative singular.
   (b) Accusative singular, neuter.
   (c) It is an adverb.
   (d) It is the 3rd person singular, imperfect subjunctive active of faciō. It is used here in a purpose clause after ut in historic sequence.
   (e) dīxērunt.
   (f) spectāret.
   (g) It is in apposition to Pīsōnem.
   (h) Prepositions are regularly omitted before towns and small islands.
   (i) It is necessary because the senators are living beings, rather than inanimate objects.
   (j) It is the present participle of timeō; it means fearing.

# Exercise 6.8

(i) fortēs cīvēs magna praemia petīvērunt.
(ii) laetī iuvenēs bonōs nūntiōs legēbant.

# Exercise 6.9

Acrisius, King of Argos, did not have any sons, but he had one daughter, Danae: he therefore asked the oracle, 'Shall I be able to have a son?' The priestess answered, 'You will not be able to have a son, and your grandson will kill you.' When Acrisius heard this, he shut his daughter in a prison, whose doors were made of bronze. There she was guarded by savage dogs. But Jupiter, who loved her, being turned into a golden shower, reached Danae and she gave birth to Perseus. When Acrisius learnt this he was extremely angry and he shut Danae with her son in a wooden chest; and he threw the chest into the sea. It approached the island Seriphus; and there it was caught by a fisherman in a net. When he opened the chest, he found the mother and the son still alive. He took them to his brother Polydectes, the king of the island. And he (Polydectes) brought up Perseus in his house.

    (a) Acrisius had one child.
    (b) It was distinctly gloomy.
    (c) It made Acrisius shut his daughter in a prison.
    (d) He loved her.
    (e) He turned himself into a golden shower.
    (f) The priestess had prophesied that his grandson would kill him.
    (g) He shut Danae and her son in a wooden chest and threw it into the sea.
    (h) It refers to arca, the chest.
    (i) He found the mother and the son still alive.
    (j) He took them to his brother Polydectes, King of Seriphus.

# Exercise 6.10

When Perseus was a young man, he defended his mother against Polydectes, who wished to marry her. But when he (Polydectes) seemed to wish to marry Hippodamia, Perseus was very happy and said to him, 'I shall give you a gift for your betrothal, (namely) the head of the Gorgon Medusa. Polydectes also was very happy because Perseus had undertaken a most difficult task. Medusa had serpents instead of hair, and very huge teeth, and a protruding tongue; those men who saw her head were turned into stones. Minerva therefore gave the young man a shield which reflected everything. Mercury gave him an adamantine sickle which was able to cut off the head. He also had to have winged sandals, a huge bag, and a helmet which made those by whom it was worn invisible. The Stygian nymphs guarded all these things: the Graeae alone knew the place in which these (nymphs) lived; they (the Graeae) were three sisters who had only one eye and one tooth.

# Exercise 6.11

Perseus took the eye of the Graeae and forced them to mention the place in which the Stygian nymphs lived. He received from them all the things that he wished to have. Then he cut off the head of Medusa while she was sleeping and placed it in the bag. With the help of the winged sandals, he escaped from her sisters; and while he was flying, he caught sight of a most beautiful woman, bound in chains. A most cruel monster of the sea wished to devour her; but Perseus cut off the head of the monster and carried the woman Andromeda with him. He showed the head of Medusa to all those who were obstructing him; and they were all turned into stones. At last he came to Seriphus. There, Polydectes had not married Hippodamia, and was forcing Danae to marry him; but Perseus showed the head of Medusa to him and to all those who were giving him help. Then he married Andromeda and sailed to Argos, and there accidentally killed Acrisius, his grandfather, with a discus; for it was this that had once been predicted. Finally Perseus was king in the Argolis.

(a) It is the 3rd person singular, perfect (past) tense of volō = I wish. The infinitive is velle.

(b) It is the perfect (past) tense of pōnō.

(c) Ablative singular; with the help of.

(d) pulcherrimam (line 7) = very beautiful; crūdēlissimum (line 9) = very cruel;

(e) While he was flying.

(f) With him(self).

(g) It tells us that Seriphus was a small island, since there is no preposition in front of it.

(h) nōn dūcēbat.

(i) It is in apposition to it.

(j) Pluperfect passive.

# Exercise 6.12

(i)  omnēs dominī trīstēs servōs saevīs vulneribus pūnīvērunt.

(ii) fessae puellae facilia itinera amant.

# Crossword

| ¹P | ²E | ³R | ⁴S | ⁵U | A | ⁶D | ⁷E | N | ⁸T |
|----|----|----|----|----|----|----|----|----|----|
| ⁹E | X | I | T | E | ■ | ¹⁰I | X | ■ | U |
| ¹¹D | I | D | O | ■ | ¹²S | C | I | ¹³M | U |
| I | ■ | E | ■ | ¹⁴R | U | E | T | I | S |
| ¹⁵B | ¹⁶A | S | ¹⁷I | O | ■ | ¹⁸S | I | T | ■ |
| ¹⁹U | M | ■ | ²⁰I | M | ²¹E | ■ | ²²S | T | ²³A |
| ²⁴S | I | ²⁵C | ■ | ²⁶A | R | ²⁷E | ■ | ²⁸A | F |
| ■ | ²⁹S | U | ³⁰A | ³¹U | X | ³²O | R | E |  |
| ³³V | I | R | T | ³⁴U | S | ■ | D | ■ | S |
| ³⁵A | T | R | I | A | ■ | ³⁶M | E | ³⁷O | S |
| T | ■ | ³⁸I | T | ■ | ³⁹C | E | U | R | I |
| ⁴⁰E | A | S | O | T | I | O | S | A | S |

# Chapter 7

## Exercise 7.1

1. superāvisse
2. līberāvisse
3. dēlēvisse
4. habuisse
5. vīdisse
6. dēfendisse
7. ruisse
8. cōnsūmpsisse
9. vēnisse
10. pūnīvisse

## Exercise 7.2

1. dīxisse
2. laudāvisse
3. fēcisse
4. vēnisse
5. iūvisse
6. bibisse
7. respondisse
8. dormīvisse
9. cōnspexisse
10. timuisse

## Exercise 7.3

| Singular | Plural | Singular | Plural | Singular | Plural |
|----------|--------|----------|--------|----------|--------|
| exercitus | exercitūs | portus | portūs | manus | manūs |
| exercitus | exercitūs | portus | portūs | manus | manūs |
| exercitum | exercitūs | portum | portūs | manum | manūs |
| exercitūs | exercituum | portūs | portuum | manūs | manuum |
| exercituī | exercitibus | portuī | portibus | manuī | manibus |
| exercitū | exercitibus | portū | portibus | manū | manibus |

## Exercise 7.4

1. At last the leader has arrived in the city with his army.
2. The king ordered his army to fight bravely with the enemy.
3. We all sailed into the harbour safe(ly).
4. In harbours there are many ships and many sailors.
5. O slave, what are you carrying in your hand? Is it really gold?
6. That girl has very beautiful hands.
7. Two armies were attacking this city in order to punish the wicked citizens.
8. In one town there was a crowd of armies.

## Exercise 7.5

1. multae nāvēs in parvō portū relictae erant.
2. mīlitibus ut gladiōs manibus ferrent imperāvimus.
3. ut nāvēs in portum nāvigantēs vidērēmus, ibi mānsimus.
4. in hōc exercitū mīlitēs pessimī sunt.

5. multae nāvēs ā multīs locīs in illōs portūs nāvigant.
6. dum cum hōc iuvene pugnābat, suās/eius manūs spectābat. (suās refers to his own hands; eius refers to the young man's hands.)
7. rēx ducī ut exercituī aurum daret imperāvit.
8. hōrum exercituum mīlitēs fortissimī sunt.

# Exercise 7.6

1. vidērī = to be seen/to seem
2. cōnsūmī = to be eaten
3. vulnerārī = to be wounded
4. pūnīrī = to be punished
5. interficī = to be killed
6. There is no present infinitive passive of faciō
7. cōnspicī = to be caught sight of
8. custōdīrī = to be guarded
9. gerī = to be waged
10. laudārī = to be praised

# Exercise 7.7

1. (a) They handed them over so that the nurses might look after them.
   (b) The result was that they frequently loved the children more than the parents did.
   (c) She was so miserable because she had fallen in love with her step-son.
   (d) Her nurse tried to assuage her grief.
   (e) She was washing his foot.
   (f) It had been inflicted by a boar.
   (g) She was so familiar with it because she had often bathed the leg in the past.
   (h) They were overjoyed.
   (i) She acted secretly because Domitian had been so unpopular.
   (j) He belonged to the gēns Flāvia, the Flavian family.

2. Both Greek and Roman parents used to hand over their children to nurses in order that they might look after them; those nurses often used to love those boys and girls more than their parents (did). In the play the *Hippolytus*, which Euripides wrote, when Phaedra had fallen in love with her step-son Hippolytus, she was greatly affected with shame and wretchedness. Her nurse tried to soften her grief. In the *Odyssey* of Homer, when Ulysses, disguised as a beggar, finally returned to his home after twenty years, Euryclea the nurse, washing his foot, immediately recognised a scar once inflicted by a boar and shouted, 'You are Ulysses!' Ecloge and Alexandra, Nero's nurses, and Acte, whom he had loved, laid to rest his remains in the monument of the family of the *gens Domitia*. Phyllis, the nurse of Domitian, who was to the senate the most hateful of emperors, conducted his funeral in her home in the suburbs and secrelty brought his remains into the temple of the *gens Flavia*.

3. (a) Imperfect subjunctive.
   (b) Ablative; it ends in a long 'ā'.
   (c) It is accusative plural, after post. It is indeclinable.
   (d) It is in apposition to it.
   (e) It is the present participle; it means 'washing'.
   (f) We have ab because a boar is a living agent.
   (g) It is dative singular of senātus; it is 4th declension; the genitive singular is senātūs.
   (h) It is the superlative; more hateful = odiōsior.
   (i) Accusative singular.
   (j) (i) īnferre; (ii) intulisse.

# Exercise 7.8

1. laudātus, -a, -um esse = to have been praised
2. dēlētus, -a, -um esse = to have been destroyed
3. ductus, -a, -um esse = to have been led
4. mōtus, -a, -um esse = to have been moved
5. positus, -a, -um esse = to have been placed
6. custōdītus, -a, -um esse = to have been guarded
7. cōnspectus, -a, -um esse = to have been caught sight of
8. missus, -a, -um esse = to have been sent
9. territus, -a, -um esse = to have been frightened
10. inventus, -a, -um esse = to have been found

# Exercise 7.9

1. The queen says that her maid-servants are singing.
2. The leader announces that the soldiers are fighting badly.
3. This young man is reading that the enemy are approaching.
4. Does not the teacher believe that the boys are working well?
5. I discover that all my money is absent.
6. We reply that the little girls are sleeping.
7. The masters are shouting that the slaves are running slowly.
8. I tell you that the king is departing from the city.
9. They hear that their mother is now arriving.
10. You write that your children are walking to the river.

# Exercise 7.10

1. hostēs fugere dīcō.
2. cīvēs agricolās in agrīs labōrāre respondent.
3. fēminās discēdere invenīmus.
4. hic puer mīlitēs venīre clāmat.
5. filiōs suōs celeriter currere mihi scrībit.
6. hostēs redīre legit.
7. senēs semper in urbe manēre crēdunt.
8. cōpiās nostrās in proelium festīnāre nūntiat.
9. puerōs in templum ambulāre audīmus.
10. quis nōbīs equōs cantāre nārrat?

# Exercise 7.11

1. He says that my mother has arrived.
2. The boys shout that our soldiers have conquered.
3. I hear that the girl was wandering through the fields.
4. Who believes that our forces have fled?
5. Do you reply that the old men hurried into the city?
6. The teachers are discovering that the boys worked badly.
7. I read that the enemy had then approached the city.
8. He tells the soldier that the boys and girls have played in the street.
9. He writes that all the women remained in the town.
10. The leader announces that the enemy suddenly departed.

# Exercise 7.12

1. hostēs celeriter fūgisse dīcit.
2. ducem redīsse crēdō.
3. magistrum quārtā hōrā discessisse respondent.
4. mihi puellās cantāvisse dīcit.
5. rēx mīlitēs nostrōs vīcisse nūntiat.
6. magistrum advēnisse audīmus.
7. animālia per viās errāvisse legit.
8. servōs ad montēs festīnāvisse inveniunt.
9. scrībisne cīvēs in urbe mānsisse?
10. agricolae nautās ad īnsulam nāvigāvisse clāmant.

# Exercise 7.13

1. He said that all those men were returning.
2. Did you not announce that the young men were present?
3. The masters replied that their slaves had hurried.
4. The leader shouted that the enemy were approaching.
5. I heard that you were in the city.
6. He wrote to me that his army had fought bravely.
7. We believed that those men were being wounded.
8. He discovered that the soldiers had stood in the road.
9. They told us that the city was being attacked.
10. I read that the leader was being wounded by the enemy.

# Exercise 7.14

1. nautās in īnsulā esse dīxērunt.
2. exercitūs nostrōs bene pugnāre nūntiāvit.
3. ducem prope templum stāre audīvī.
4. rēgī cīvēs fūgisse scrīpsit.
5. incolae hostēs prope oppidum esse clāmābant.
6. vōbīs senēs dormīre nārrāvimus.
7. multum cibum cōnsūmī crēdidī.
8. bellum parārī respondit.
9. lēgistīne/lēgistisne agricolās in agrōs discessisse?
10. puerōs in viā esse invēnit.

# Exercise 7.15

1. We hear that the ship has been destroyed.
2. The leader announced that the enemy had been conquered.
3. I say that the maid-servants have been called by the queen.
4. We replied that the old men were wretched.
5. They discovered that those girls were very beautiful.
6. Did you really believe that your city was great?
7. I have read that those horses are strong.
8. The soldiers shout that the weapons have been collected.
9. I told the citizens that the walls had been defended.
10. He wrote to me that rewards had been sought by the soldiers.

# Exercise 7.16

1. dīxistīne/dīxistisne mulierēs servātās esse?
2. lēgistīne/lēgistisne novōs mūrōs aedificātōs esse?
3. servōs līberātōs esse respondērunt.
4. gladiōs mōtōs esse invēnī.
5. dīxistīne nōbīs puellās optimās fuisse?
6. omnia arma trādita esse crēdidī.
7. senēs fessōs esse scrīpsērunt.
8. magister malōs puerōs pūnītōs esse nūntiāvit.
9. nautae agricolās superātōs esse clāmāvērunt.
10. num cōpiās nostrās captās esse audīvistī?

# Exercise 7.17

1. I shall say that our soldiers have not been conquered.
2. They said that the city had not been defended.
3. I say that the leader is not brave.
4. That man says that our city is not very beautiful.
5. I say that the teachers have not punished the boys.
6. I believe that the cruel soldiers have wounded the tired old men.
7. I said that the farmers were not in the fields.
8. We announced that the young men were defending the women.
9. I discovered that wicked men were wounding the horses.
10. We say that the parents had not been left with their children in the city.

# Exercise 7.18

1. hostēs fortēs esse negāvit.
2. mūrōs aedificātōs esse negāvit.
3. senēs iuvenem in templō esse negāvērunt.
4. iuvenēs mulierēs dēfendere crēdidimus.
5. parentēs līberōs suōs pūnīvisse negāvī.
6. num dominum servōs suōs līberāvisse crēdis?
7. hostēs Rōmānōs vincere posse negāvit.
8. urbem captam esse negāvērunt
9. num puerōs iuvenēs superāvisse crēdidistī/crēdidistis?
10. dux cīvibus poētam sapientem esse dīxit.

# Exercise 7.19

1. hostēs ā proeliō fugere dīxit.
   He said that the enemy were fleeing from the battle.

2. puerōs ā magistrīs laudārī dīxit.
   He said that the boys were being praised by the teachers.

3. multōs cīvēs ā mīlitibus occīsōs esse dīxit.
   He said that many citizens had been killed by the soldiers.

4. omnēs fēminās ex urbe discessisse dīxit.
   He said that all the women had departed form the city.

5. puellās librum lēgisse dīxit.
   He said that the girls had read the book.

6. pulchrās mulierēs in oppidō habitāre dīxit.
   He said that beautiful women were living in the town.

7. bonōs agricolās in agrīs labōrāre dīxit.
   He said that good farmers were working in the fields.

8. fortēs nautās circum īnsulam nāvigāvisse dīxit.
   He said that brave sailors had sailed round the island.

9. bonōs puerōs ā parentibus amārī dīxit.
   He said that good boys were loved by their parents.

10. parvam puellam in urbe relictam esse dīxit.
    He said that a little girl had been left in the city.

# Exercise 7.20

1. Who announced that you had built the wall?
2. The old men replied to us that they had done great things.
3. Do they really tell that they have been conquered?
4. They shouted that he was being killed.
5. A messenger read to me that you (women) had been saved.
6. We believe that we ourselves have overcome everyone.
7. He discovered that this itself had been done.
8. Do you really hear that we are being overcome?
9. Why do you say that you yourself are very wise?
10. They wrote that they were remaining in the harbour.

# Exercise 7.21

1. mē ipsum bonum mīlitem esse dīxī.
2. dux mihi sē diū pugnāvisse dīxit.
3. vōs ipsōs optimōs cīvēs esse nūntiāvistis.
4. vōs fortiter pugnāre clāmāvērunt.
5. nōnne hostēs ā vōbīs victōs esse audīvērunt?
6. eōs celeriter fūgisse respondimus.
7. sē ipsam et pulchram et sapientem esse crēdidit.
8. sē ipsōs ex portū nāvigāre scrīpsērunt.
9. eum audācissimum iuvenem esse invēnī.
10. eum bonās rēs fēcisse lēgit.

# Exercise 7.22

1. rēgī tē advēnisse dīxī.
2. agricola ventum mūrōs dēlēre clāmat.
3. sē ipsum librōs lēgisse mihi respondit.
4. sē ipsam sapientem esse lēgit.
5. dominus servōs bene labōrāre crēdidit.
6. dux cīvibus hostēs victōs esse nūntiāvit.
7. iuvenibus fēlīcibus iter facile esse scrīpsī.
8. magistrō puellam inventam esse respondit.
9. rēx ducēs omnēs fortissimōs esse scrīpsit.
10. laetus senex nōs appropinquāre audīvit.

# Exercise 7.23

1. Manual
2. Port
3. Gradual
4. Domestic
5. Negate
6. Oration

# Exercise 7.24

1. novum oppidum ā crūdēlibus hostibus oppugnābātur.
2. omnēs puellae librōs suōs in urbe legēbant.
3. bonī agricolae in hīs agrīs labōrābant.
4. magistrī fessī bona verba puerōrum et puellārum audiunt.
5. fortēs iuvenēs trāns viam ambulābant.
6. malī mīlitēs ā duce pūniēbantur.
7. puellae cum puerīs in agrō lūdēbant.
8. omnia animālia ab altīs montibus discessērunt.
9. nautae saevī omnem aquam bibērunt et cibum omnem cōnsūmpsērunt.
10. laetus senex verba sapientia iuvenī scrībit.

# Exercise 7.25

1. (a) He made things more cheerful by pouring out nectar for all of them.
   (b) The sight of him bustling about through their abodes.
   (c) He was the leader of the Trojans.
   (d) He wanted to lift him up.
   (e) The child wept in fear of his father's helmet and hid himself in the bosom of his nurse.
   (f) They laughed.
   (g) He was no longer afraid because his father had put his crested helmet on the ground.
   (h) He remembered that he could order his slaves to kill his guests.
   (i) Many benches were knocked over because a member of the audience was so fat.
   (j) Claudius kept remembering this incident and it made him laugh.

2.   In the *Iliad* of Homer, after Jupiter and Juno had quarrelled with each other, Vulcan, their son, made peace
     between them and poured out nectar, the wine of the gods, for all the gods. Then, when the gods saw him
     bustling about through their abodes, they gave forth unquenchable (peals of) laughter. In the *Iliad* again,
     when Hector, the leader of the Trojans, returned from the battle to his wife and baby son and wished to lift
     him up in his hands, the baby, fearing his crested helmet, wept and hid himself in the bosom of his nurse.
     Then the father and the mother laughed, and Hector placed his helmet on the ground and caressed his son.
     We have already read that Caligula had been unable to abstain from laughter when dining; for he
     remembered that he could order his slaves to kill his guests. While Claudius was reading his work to a very
     large number of people, many benches were knocked over by the fatness of a member of the audience;
     Claudius remembered that this had happened again and again and, being overcome with laughter, read his
     work to the end with difficulty.

3.   (a) Dative plural of deus; vocative singular: deus.
     (b) Present participle.
     (c) Accusative plural.
     (d) redībit.
     (e) Volcānus, filius eōrum (line 2) = Vulcan, their son;
         nectar, deōrum vīnum (lines 3-4) = nectar, the wine of the gods;
         Hector, dux Troiānōrum (lines 6-7) = Hector, leader of the Trojans;
         filiumque īnfantem (lines 7-8) = and his son, a baby.
     (f) sinuī.
     (g) Accusative singular. Genitive singular: operis; it means work.
     (h) It is in the present tense after dum because while something was happening (Claudius reading his work),
         some new thing happened (the knocking over of the benches). See Pupil's book, page 69.
     (i) It is present because the 'e' is not long.
     (j) Perfect infinitive active; it is in an indirect statement after meminerat: Claudius remembered that this
         had happened.

# Chapter 8

## Exercise 8.1

1.   The leader was urging the soldiers to attack the town bravely.
2.   The mothers urged their daughters to behave themselves well.
3.   The teacher is encouraging the boys while they run.
4.   I shall try to do this work.
5.   Will you not try to cross that river?
6.   She said that she had tried in vain to work in the field.
7.   The same teacher will always encourage the horses, the boys, the girls and the sailors with the same words.
8.   I encouraged those women to sing well in the temple.
9.   Oh young men, did you really try to defend the old men?
10.  Do you not always encourage those who try to write well?

## Exercise 8.2

1.   hōs omnēs agricolās hortārī volō.
2.   cīvēs ut urbem fortiter dēfenderent hortābāmur.
3.   omnia bene facere cōnātī erant.
4.   circum īnsulam nāvigāre cōnāmur.
5.   num puerōs ut illud difficile iter facerent hortātus es?
6.   amīcum meum nē Rōmam īret hortātus sum.
7.   omnēs librum dē hīs rēbus scrībere cōnābimur.
8.   perterritās fēminās hortārī frūstrā cōnāmur.
9.   pater fīlium suum ut viam hīc trānsīret hortātus est.
10.  cīvēs, quamquam dux eōs ut fugerent hortābātur, in oppidō manēbant et pugnāre cōnābantur.

## Exercise 8.3

| 1. monuissem | 3. audīvissem | 5. bibissem | 7. fēcissem | 9. vīdissem |
|---|---|---|---|---|
| monuissēs | audīvissēs | bibissēs | fēcissēs | vīdissēs |
| monuisset | audīvisset | bibisset | fēcisset | vīdisset |
| monuissēmus | audīvissēmus | bibissēmus | fēcissēmus | vīdissēmus |
| monuissētis | audīvissētis | bibissētis | fēcissētis | vīdissētis |
| monuissent | audīvissent | bibissent | fēcissent | vīdissent |

| 2. rēxissem | 4. līberāvissem | 6. pūnīvissem | 8. appropinquāvissem | 10. vēnissem |
|---|---|---|---|---|
| rēxissēs | līberāvissēs | pūnīvissēs | appropinquāvissēs | vēnissēs |
| rēxisset | līberāvisset | pūnīvisset | appropinquāvisset | vēnisset |
| rēxissēmus | līberāvissēmus | pūnīvissēmus | appropinquāvissēmus | vēnissēmus |
| rēxissētis | līberāvissētis | pūnīvissētis | appropinquāvissētis | vēnissētis |
| rēxissent | līberāvissent | pūnīvissent | appropinquāvissent | vēnissent |

# Exercise 8.4

1. When they had caught sight of the enemy, the old men fled.
2. When the teacher had heard the boys he praised them all.
3. After having drunk the wine, the young men slept.
4. After the soldiers had escaped from the danger, the leader punished them.
5. After having heard the words of the messenger, I was very greatly afraid.
6. After having read that book, he wished to read another.
7. When we had made that journey, we were extremely tired.
8. After having defended the city well, you were praised by everybody.
9. Why did you not greet me when I had finally arrived?
10. After having run as quickly as possible through the fields, I entered the temple.

# Exercise 8.5

1. parentēs, cum vōcēs filiōrum audīvissent, laetī fuērunt.
2. senēs, cum hostēs vīdissent, timuērunt.
3. hunc dominum, cum bonum servum līberāvisset, omnēs laudābant.
4. iuvenēs, cum urbem fortiter dēfendissent, ab omnibus laudātī sunt.
5. magister, cum optimīs puerīs praemia dedisset, eōs ut lūderent hortātus est.
6. cum omnia ex urbe cēpissent, nihil relictum est.
7. virī, cum mulierēs cibum parāvissent, eum cōnsūmpsērunt.
8. iuvenēs, cum senēs cīvēs dē perīculō monuissent, rīsērunt.
9. omnēs parentēs, cum ducēs puerōs in urbem redūxissent, laetī fuērunt.
10. cum arma in oppidum tulisset, quam celerrimē discessit.

# Exercise 8.6

1. (a) He urged him not to defend Troy and to found a new city for the Trojan gods.
   (b) Because, as his mother, she wished to support her son. Agamemnon had just offended him.
   (c) She wished them to recognise how much they needed Achilles.
   (d) No it was not true.
   (e) He was told by the dream that the gods and goddesses were all in agreement about this.
   (f) It told him not to go on sleeping.
   (g) He was very happy because he thought that he was about to capture Troy.
   (h) One was true and the other was false.
   (i) We learn that he went in too readily for wishful thinking.
   (j) He failed to overcome the Trojans.

2. We have recently read about the dream of Aeneas, in which Hector urged him not to defend Troy and to found a new city for the Trojan gods; this dream was truthful. In the *Iliad* of Homer, when King Agamemnon had rashly offended Achilles, Thetis, the mother of Achilles, who was the bravest of the Greeks, begged Jupiter, the king of the gods, to help the Trojans and to harm the Greeks; for Achilles had departed from the battle in a great rage. Jupiter therefore sent a destructive dream to Agamemnon; to this dream he said the following: 'Go, oh destructive dream, go and say these words to Agamemnon: "Today you will capture the city of Troy; for the gods and goddesses do not disagree any more among themselves; arise therefore, arm your Greeks, and you will overcome your enemies; for thus has Jupiter decided."' The dream went and encouraged Agamemnon in this way. 'Do not sleep,' it said, and it added the words of Jupiter. Agamemnon arose, very happy, and when he had called together all the leaders he told them about the dream. The dream however was most deceitful and, after having behaved most unwisely, not only did Agamemnon not overcome the Trojans but he was also himself nearly overcome by a very great danger.

3.    (a) et deābus.
      (b) It is in apposition to it.
          Agamemnōn, rēx (line 6) = Agamemnon, the king;
          Iovem, rēgem deōrum (line 7) = Jupiter, the king of the gods;
          urbem Troiam (line 12) = the city Troy;
      (c) mittō, mittere, mīsī, missum = I send
      (d) Vocative singular; perniciōsum.
      (e) It is the singular imperative of dīcō; the form is irregular in having dropped the final 'e' (like dūc, fer and fac).
      (f) The singular imperative of armō, armāre = I arm.
      (g) dormīre nōlīte!
      (h) ducum.
      (i) tamen is generally not written first word in a clause or sentence. The same is true of igitur (line 9, 14).
      (j) gereret.

# Exercise 8.7

1.    I have spoken with the teacher concerning the prizes which we had decided to give to the boys and girls.
2.    Were you not following the young men to the mountains?
3.    After having prepared everything, we set out from the city as quickly as possible.
4.    The leader will speak about many things.
5.    It is very difficult to follow swift animals.
6.    The old men had already set out from the city yesterday.
7.    All the women tried to sing well.
8.    Why were you encouraging the boys to cross the road?

# Exercise 8.8

1.    cum omnia fēcissēmus, omnēs nē timērent hortātī sumus.
2.    quamquam cum senibus loquī cōnābāmur, respondēre nōbīs nōn poterant.
3.    fēminae, quod senēs ex oppidō secūtae erant, in agrīs erant.
4.    quis mēcum ad pulcherrimam terram proficīscētur?
5.    facilius est sequī quam dūcere.
6.    cum iam redīssēmus, proficīscēbāminī.
7.    negāvit sē puerōs ex templō secūtam esse.
8.    dominī sē cum puerīs locūtōs esse respondērunt et cum servīs loquī.

# Exercise 8.9

1.    The citizens heard the leader saying many things.
2.    Did you see the soldiers setting out to the battle?
3.    Give help to the boy who is trying to do his work.
4.    We heard the voice of the teacher who were encouraging the boys.
5.    I heard the shouts of the young men, who were following us.
6.    The farmers were fighting with the sailors who were trying to terrify the horses.
7.    We praised the little girls who were trying to sing well.
8.    The boys were punished by the teachers who were saying many things.
9.    I caught sight of a crowd of old men who were setting out from the city.
10.   I saw the leader urging on the soldiers who were following the army of the enemy.

# Exercise 8.10

1. nūntiōs loquentēs audiēbat.
2. hoc opus est puerī omnia bene facere cōnantis.
3. cibum puellīs nōs sequentibus dedimus.
4. illa arma mīlitum sunt proficīscentium.
5. in eōdem locō stetit, puerōs et puellās hortāns.
6. dominus servōs bene labōrāre cōnantēs laudābat.
7. iuvenēs ex urbe proficīscentēs laetissimī erant.
8. dōna pulchra uxōribus dedimus coniugēs suōs sequentibus.
9. ubi sunt librī puerōrum et puellārum dē patriā nostrā loquentium?
10. nōs omnēs ducem in mediā urbe loquentem laudāvimus.

# Exercise 8.11

1. Tomorrow, having set out from the city we shall make a journey to the mountains.
2. Having encouraged the boys to run as quickly as possible the teacher was reading a book.
3. Having followed the enemy to the sea they forced them to fight.
4. Having tried in vain to seize the town, the enemy departed, both tired and angry.
5. The courage of the soldiers, who have already set out, is very great.
6. After they had spoken with the citizens, the messengers departed.
7. Having followed the bad men to the mountains, we found gold.
8. We did not give these things to the young men who had set out.
9. Everyone praised the teacher who had encouraged the boys and girls well.
10. What did you say to the old man, who had tried to escape the danger?

# Exercise 8.12

1. quis hās rēs Caesarī nūntiābit, ex urbe profectō?
2. hī librī puerōrum sunt dē proeliīs locūtōrum.
3. magister, puellam ut cantāret hortātus, laetus erat.
4. dux mīlitēs exercitum hostium secūtōs laudāvit.
5. optimum praemium mulierī coniugem suum servāre cōnātae dedī.
6. ex īnsulā profectus redīre voluī.
7. nōlī/nōlīte iuvenēs laudāre opus suum facere nōn cōnātōs.
8. hī sapientēs multa dē multīs rēbus locūtī nihil fēcērunt.
9. mīlitēs agricolās in agrum secūtī multōs equōs ibi invēnērunt.
10. iuvenēs senēs ut fortēs essent hortātī fūgērunt.

# Exercise 8.13

1. We sent armies to conquer the enemy.
2. They were running through the fields, in order to arrive at the city more quickly.
3. Many bad men tried to terrify me as I was speaking all these things.
4. The master had sent a savage slave to punish the others.
5. Why are you following us as we go home?
6. There were many beautiful women present.
7. The enemy had destroyed the walls in order to enter the city more easily.
8. We sent girls into the temple to sing there.
9. Having set out today to the mountains, the young men have returned.
10. The citizens had stood near the wall, in order to see the battle better.

# Exercise 8.14

1. bonī puerī ā laetō magistrō laudātī sunt.
2. crūdēlis dominus trīstēs servōs pūniēbat.
3. multum cibum cōnsūmēbāmus.
4. parvae puellae per magnum agrum currēbant.
5. nautae superbī in magnīs nāvibus per multa maria nāvigāvērunt.
6. dē monte, quō melius oppidum dēfenderētis, vēnistis.
7. post longam noctem cīvēs in urbem mīsimus quī arma parārent.
8. rēgīna ancillās mīsit quae cibum invenīrent.
9. ducēs mīlitēs mīsērunt quī hostēs superārent.
10. fessī senēs, quō facilius proelium spectārent, in altīs mūrīs ambulābant.

# Exercise 8.15

1. (a) It brings rest to men.
   (b) He was unable to sleep because he was disturbed about his father.
   (c) They both feared losing the man they loved.
   (d) He had decided to depart because Mercury had warned him to sail to Italy.
   (e) Everyone laughed because Claudius rubbed his face vigorously with slippers.
   (f) He was angry because Vespasian fell asleep while he was singing.
   (g) He punished him by sending him to Judaea where war was being waged.
   (h) He was made emperor by the soldiers under his command.
   (i) Nero would have been extremely annoyed because the 'punishment' of Vespasian led to his becoming emperor.
   (j) He was a good and wise emperor.

2. The Greeks used to say that sleep was sweet; the Romans used to say that it was a gift of the gods; for it brings rest to men; but Homer says that the son of Ulysses, disturbed about his father, was not able to sleep. Medea, deeply moved on account of the dangers by which Jason, whom she loved, was surrounded, was not able to sleep. And Dido was not able to sleep while sleep ruled everywhere; for Aeneas, whom she loved, warned by Mercury to sail to Italy, had decided to depart. Before he was made emperor, slippers were placed around the hands of Claudius as he was sleeping; and immediately on waking up he rubbed his face vigorously with them; and everyone laughed. In Greece, Vespasian fell asleep while Nero was singing; Nero was very angry and sent him to Judaea; for a very savage war was being waged there; and afterwards, when Nero and three other emperors had died, Vespasian, having been made emperor by the legions of which he was leader, governed the state well and wisely for ten years.

3. (a) 3rd person singular, present tense of ferō, ferre, tulī, lātum = I carry, bear, bring.
   (b) filī.
   (c) Past participle passive.
   (d) poterit.
   (e) In lines 7-8 dum is followed by the imperfect because she was unable to sleep throughout the time that sleep ruled everywhere else. In lines 14-15 dum is followed by the present tense, because Vespasian fell asleep at a particular moment while Nero was singing.
   (f) It is pluperfect. The subjunctive is cōnstituisset.
   (g) Genitive singular, or nominative, vocative or accusative plural. Here it is accusative plural.
   (h) antequam (= before) is a conjunction introducing a subordinate clause, and must therefore always be followed (in sense) by a verb.
   (i) saevius.
   (j) 3rd person plural, pluperfect subjunctive of pereō; cum + pluperfect subjunctive = when, after.

# Chapter 9

## Exercise 9.1

1. The house of that citizen is very beautiful.
2. The houses of those citizens are very beautiful.
3. Whose is this house?
4. I shall soon approach your house.
5. Oh very good house, who lives in you?
6. The boys said that there were little animals in those houses.
7. The leader ordered the old men to go out of those houses and go into these houses.
8. When my son had seen his friend's house he approached it.
9. Although this man is very famous, he does not have his own house.
10. Is there really a house in this town better than our house?

## Exercise 9.2

1. ducis domus altissima est.
2. illae domūs illōrum senum sunt.
3. potesne clārōrum cīvium domōs vidēre?
4. haec domus omnium domuum optima est.
5. puerōs in illīs domibus esse negāvit.
6. quis domum in quā habitātis aedificāvit?
7. nihil in illā domō relictum est.
8. rēx mīlitibus ut ducum domōs dēlērent imperāvit.
9. quis huius ingentis domūs dominus est?
10. quis nostrae domuī appropinquat?

## Exercise 9.3

1. When they heard these words, they fled to Caesar's home.
2. That tired woman has returned home down from the mountain.
3. Was your father at home yesterday?
4. He said that he wished to remain in his own home.
5. All the slaves have departed from home.
6. I am going home as quickly as possible because wicked young men are playing in the streets.
7. I saw a man going to my mother's home.
8. Seek me in the home of my friend.

## Exercise 9.4

1. domī sum hodiē et domī crās manēbō.
2. suam domum redīre vult.
3. ut tempestātem effugerent domum currēbant.
4. domō profectī ad flūmen festīnāvimus.
5. dominum nostrum domum euntem vīdī.

6. nōlīte mātris meae domī clāmāre!
7. servī domō ad agrōs discessērunt.
8. amīcus meus subitō frātris suī domum ierat.

# Exercise 9.5

1. The food having been prepared, the boys returned home.
2. While the girls were singing, the teachers were happy.
3. While the teacher was approaching, the young men fled.
4. Our books having been left at home, we walked to the fields.
5. Were you really able to sleep while the enemy were attacking the town?
6. A high wall having been built around the city, the old men believed that they were safe.
7. While the soldiers were drinking wine the citizens remained at home.
8. The city of the enemy having been captured, the Romans behaved themselves well.
9. When the horse had been wounded, the farmers were very angry.
10. When the ship had been destroyed, the sailors were very unhappy.

# Exercise 9.6

1. rīdente magistrō, puerī laetī nōn erant.
2. senibus bene dēfēnsīs, rēx iuvenēs fortissimōs fuisse dīxit.
3. laudātīs puellīs, puerī sē quoque bene fēcisse dīxērunt.
4. appropinquante diē, omnēs incolae lūcem clāriōrem vidēbant.
5. magnīs mūrīs aedificātīs, urbs tūtissima erat.
6. multīs armīs ducī datīs, cīvēs sē pugnāre velle clāmāvērunt.
7. pugnantibus mīlitibus, iter difficile fēcistis.
8. custōde interfectō, nēmō viam custōdiēbat.
9. hōc puerō pulchra dōna accipiente, ille puer nihil accēpit.
10. multīs sagittīs iactīs, hostēs superātōs esse crēdidērunt.

# Exercise 9.7

1. Having entered the city, they were walking through the streets.
2. Aeneas suffered many things in wars.
3. The enemy were advancing slowly across the mountains.
4. On this journey many will die.
5. Who will allow these men to enter the city?
6. Yesterday twenty-seven soldiers died.
7. Why do you allow no one to go out of the temple?
8. Having advanced quickly, we came to the river.

# Exercise 9.8

1. crās iter difficile ingrediar.
2. Aenēās, magna perīcula passus, Ītaliam cum dīs suīs et comitibus ingressus est.
3. cum hostēs cōnspexissēmus, ex urbe quam celerrimē ēgressī sumus.
4. ā cīvibus līberātī nautae ad portum prōgressī sunt.
5. multī mīlitēs quī nunc pugnant crās morientur.

6.  tē/vōs domī meae crūdēlem/crūdēlēs esse nōn patiar.
7.  eī omnēs, ut haec facerent, multa passī sunt.
8.  num amīcōs vestrōs morī patiēminī?

# Exercise 9.9

1.  (a) He was riding home to his parents.
    (b) No; winter was approaching and the ground was covered in snow.
    (c) He thought he saw an old man, lying on the ground, almost naked, ill and wounded.
    (d) He said that they would soon die of hunger and cold.
    (e) He was laughing because he had tricked the young man.
    (f) He wanted to wound him in order to prevent him from following him.
    (g) He appears not to have been worried by this, because he said, 'Do with me what you wish.'
    (h) He wanted him to promise not to boast about what he had done.
    (i) The young man means that people may be discouraged from offering help to a man who is really poor, in case he is a thief in disguise.
    (j) The thief returned everything to the young man and left; and after that he never again deceived or wounded or stole from anyone.

2.  I remember that my mother told me this short story. Once upon a time a young man was riding home on horseback to his parents. The winter was already approaching and the earth was covered with snow. Suddenly he caught sight of an old man lying on the ground, nearly naked, ill and wounded. 'Help me!' cried the old man, 'for I am very poor. I have a wife and children who will soon die of hunger and cold.' When the young man had immediately got down from his horse in order to bring help to the old man, he (the old man), laughing and no longer similar to an old man, having unsheathed his sword, ordered the young man to give him all his money, all his gold and all his clothes. When this was done the thief said that he wished to wound the young man in order that he should not decide to follow him. The young man said, 'Do with me what you wish to do, but promise me this one thing.' 'What?' 'Do not boast that you have done this.' 'Why not?' 'Because all those who hear this will not wish to bring help to a man who is truly very poor and he with his wife and children will die of hunger and cold.' When this had been said by the young man, the thief no longer laughing gave back all this things to the young man and departed, and after this he did not deceive men or wound them or steal their things.

3.  (a) It is an indirect statement (accusative and infinitive); the accusatives mātrem meam govern the infinitive nārrāvisse.
    (b) iuvenum. As a non-increasing noun, one would expect the genitive plural to end in –ium. It is an exception.
    (c) Present participle.
    (d) cōnspiciō, cōnspicere, cōnspexī, cōnspectum = I catch sight of.
    (e) No; the regular form would have a short 'e'.
    (f) mortuī sunt.
    (g) In line 9 ut introduces a final (purpose) clause meaning 'in order to'. In lines 10-12 ut introduces an indirect command.
    (h) 3rd person singular, pluperfect subjunctive active of dēscendō. The pluperfect subjunctive is regularly used after cum when it means 'when' or 'after'.
    (i) gladiō dēstrictō (line 10) = his sword having been unsheathed; quō factō (line 12) = which thing having been done; hōc dictō (lines 19-20) = this having been said; omnibus rēbus redditīs (lines 20-21) = all the things having been given back.
    (j) fac: 2nd person singular imperative of faciō = do! vīs: 2nd person singular, present indicative of volō = you wish.

# Exercise 9.10

1. After having conquered the enemy, the leader returned to the camp.
2. Having prepared the food, the woman ordered the boys and girls to come to her home.
3. After having built a great wall, the farmers were tired.
4. On catching sight of the teacher, the boys behaved well.
5. Having done their tasks quickly, the slaves were praised.
6. Having written a new book, the poet was happy.
7. Having made a long and difficult journey, the girls wished to sleep.
8. The old men and the young men left the town and walked through the fields.
9. The teachers punished the bad boys and departed.
10. After having ruled his cities well for many years, the king finally died.

# Exercise 9.11

1. librō lēctō novum opus ingressī sumus.
2. aurō inventō domum rediērunt.
3. cibō cōnsūmptō, dormiēbant.
4. illīs rēbus frūstrā petītīs, miserī estis.
5. dux Rōmānus, Graecīs victīs, ab omnibus laudātus est.
6. oppidō relictō per agrōs errābant.
7. dux, cīvibus laudātīs, discessit.
8. malus homō, mulieris coniuge interfectō, pūnītus est.
9. magister, eīs quī cantābant laudātīs, in templō manēbat.
10. hostēs, mūrīs dēlētīs, urbem ingressī sunt.

# Exercise 9.12

1. While reading the books, the boys said nothing.
2. Since/because the sailors were approaching, the farmers were preparing to defend themselves.
3. Since/because they believed it to be very difficult, they did not wish to undertake that journey.
4. Though this boy was very small, he used to fight bravely with big young men.
5. Since/because that king was very cruel, nobody loved him.
6. The citizens were fleeing into the fields since/because a very great storm was destroying their homes.
7. Everyone praised the boys since/because they sang well in the temple.
8. Though the winds were very savage, many citizens were walking in the streets.
9. The young men were singing while they were eating food.
10. Since/because they were drinking much wine, the young men were shouting loudly.

# Exercise 9.13

1. puellae, cum puerī in viīs lūderent, librōs suōs legēbant.
2. ancillae, cum rēgīna eās vocāret, ad eam ruēbant.
3. cum hostēs cum mīlitibus nostrīs pugnārent, domī manēbam.
4. cum vōs omnēs fugerētis, nēmō nōs dēfendēbat.
5. cum nōs ut domō exīrēmus rogāret, cum patre nostrō loquēbāmur.
6. cīvēs, cum Rōmānī urbem oppugnārent, cibum nōn habēbant.

7. cum maximus exercitus hostium adīret, nēmō fūgit.
8. puerī, cum magister eōs pūnīret, trīstēs erant.
9. mīlitēs, cum vīnum biberent, rīdēbant.
10. mīlitēs, cum multum vīnum biberent, clāmābant.

# Exercise 9.14

1. Having done their work, the girls returned home.
2. Having conquered the enemy, Caesar advanced into Gaul.
3. Having conquered the enemy, Caesar followed them to the river.
4. After the boys had been punished, the girls were frightened.
5. We ordered the young man who was approaching us to depart from the town.
6. While the teacher was approaching, the boys and girls behaved very well.
7. After eating much food, the old man wished to sleep.
8. They gave many very beautiful gifts to the woman who was singing very well.
9. After the leader had spoken, the citizens were preparing to fight with the enemy.
10. The mother of the slave who had been set free was happy.

# Exercise 9.15

1. mūrīs aedificātīs, cīvēs tūtī erant.
2. multīs domibus dēlētīs, in agrōs ambulāvimus.
3. ducēs aurum in urbe inventum habēre volēbant.
4. fēminae mīlitēs vulnerātōs iuvāre cōnābantur.
5. urbe oppugnātā, senēs ad montēs fūgērunt.
6. puellae laudātae magistrī praemium dedērunt.
7. hīs verbīs dictīs, nēmō ex oppidō discēdet.
8. omnēs, tempestāte exspectātā, domī manēbant.
9. hōs puerōs bene labōrantēs magistrī nōn pūnīvērunt.
10. nautīs urbem spectantibus, agricolae agrōs dēfendere cōnstituērunt.

# Exercise 9.16

1. Exhort (urge, encourage); hortor = I encourage.
2. Elocution (the art of speaking); loquor = I speak.
3. Immortal (not subject to death); morior, morī, mortuus sum = I die.
4. Patient (someone who is suffering); patior = I suffer.
5. Progress (advancement); prōgredior, prōgredī, prōgressus sum = I advance.
6. Consequently (following on); sequor = I follow.

# Exercise 9.17

1. When I was a boy, our soldiers used to conquer all others.
2. Who was the best of the citizens when you were a young man?
3. When that man was king, all men were wretched.
4. With Caesar as our leader, we overcame everyone.

5.   Oh boys and girls, when I am an old man, you will be fathers and mothers.
6.   Do you wish to make a journey to the river with me as your companion?
7.   When Titus was the teacher, the boys used to say nothing.
8.   When you were guard, the young men escaped.
9.   When he was emperor, we were all happy.
10.  Who ruled the inhabitants when you were a girl?

# Exercise 9.18

1.   illō rēge, nēmō laetus erat.
2.   mē puerō, multī (virī) in templō cantābant.
3.   hōc duce, omnēs hostēs vincēmus.
4.   tē iuvene, puer eram.
5.   illō prīncipe, paucī exercitūs Rōmānī vincēbantur.
6.   mē puellā, omnēs laetī erant.
7.   Aulō custōde, servī in agrīs bene labōrant.
8.   eā rēgīnā, omnēs ancillae miserae erant.
9.   tē magistrō, puerī et puellae librōs suōs legunt.
10.  mē sene, Rōma etiam clārior erit.

# Exercise 9.19

1.   (a) Everyone hated the king because he was so proud and because he punished his opponents most cruelly.
     (b) As an opponent of the king, he had been condemned to death.
     (c) The young man was told that his father was lying in bed, dying.
     (d) The young man begged the king to be allowed to visit his dying father.
     (e) The king granted this favour on condition that the young man's friend should stay in prison instead of
         him and be executed if he did not return in time.
     (f) A storm suddenly broke out, trees collapsed everywhere, his horse was wounded, rivers overflowed.
     (g) He did not believe that the young man would return home. He taunted his friend for believing that he
         would.
     (h) He thought he was stupid for having believed his friend.
     (i) trīstēs = sad.
     (j) plaudentibus omnibus = while everyone applauded.

2.   There was once a very proud king, whom everyone hated; he used to punish his opponents most cruelly.
     Among these was a young man, condemned to death: he, who was bound in prison, was due to die on an
     appointed day. A messenger told him that his father, an old man, was lying in bed, dying. That father lived
     in a distant town and had not learnt of his son's fate. His son begged the king that he might be allowed to
     visit his father. He (the king) answered, 'I allow you to go, but beforehand your friend will have to remain
     in prison and, unless you return after one month on the appointed day, he will be put to death.' Immediately
     after his best friend had been bound in the prison, the young man departed. He visited his father, and buried
     him when he died, and was hurrying home as quickly as possible. But after a strorm had suddenly broken
     out, trees had collapsed everywhere, his horse was wounded and the rivers were overflowing, he dragged
     himself home, ill and scarcely alive. Meanwhile the king used to visit his friend every day; laughing, he
     used to say to him, 'Your friend will never come; you, who believed him, are stupid.' The appointed day
     came. A block was put in place. The friend bent his head; the executioner stood near; all the citizens were
     present, sad; the hour came; the king was on the point of ordering the friend to be beheaded; and suddenly

the voice of a man was heard, crying, 'Stop. I am here. I have come home.' And the two friends embraced each other. The king, very greatly moved, said to them, while all applauded, 'Accept me, I beg you, as your third friend.'

3.    (a) It is a superlative adverb.
     (b) It is feminine because it refers to an appointed day.
     (c) It is an indirect statement (accusative and infinitive), introduced by dīxit.
     (d) It is an indirect command, introduced by ōrāvit.
     (e) 2nd person singular, future tense of redeō, redīre, rediī, reditum = I return (intrans.).
     (f) It is an ablative absolute. tempestāte coortā (line 15) = a storm having arisen; arboribus collāpsīs (lines 15-16) = trees having collapsed; equō vulnerātō (line 16) = the horse having been wounded; flūminibus redundantibus (line 17) = with the rivers overflowing; plaudentibus omnibus (line 27) = with everyone applauding.
     (g) vīset.
     (h) Accusative singular.
     (i) Present infinitive passive = to be beheaded.
     (j) vōcum; it is regular, since it increases its number of syllables (from nominative to genitive singular).

# Exercise 9.20

1.    fortēs mīlitēs ā nōbilī duce laudābantur.
2.    pulchrae puellae sacra verba cantābant.
3.    fessī senēs ad altōs montēs ambulāvērunt.
4.    perterritī nūntiī arma sua in altum mare iēcērunt.
5.    inter tēla hostium sagittae sunt et hastae.
6.    validī iuvenēs in montēs iter difficile fēcērunt.
7.    magnī equī ex agrō ad flūmen ruunt.
8.    īrātī parentēs trīstēs līberōs pūnīvērunt.
9.    fortis dux excercitum magnum in proelium dūxit.
10.   miserae mulierēs saevōrum iuvenum clāmōrēs audiēbant.

# Chapter 10

We are supplying a translation to all these stories, whether it is required or not.

## Exercise 10.1

After the death of Nero there were four emperors in one year; the first of these was Galba; he was seventy-one years old, was experienced in public life but was also very mean and very strict; he decided to take back a very large part of the gifts from the many men to whom Nero had given gifts; when he had been made emperor by the soldiers he did not give largesse to them; for he boasted that he chose soldiers, and did not buy them. He adopted Piso, who was well known to few people, and not even then was the accustomed largesse given to the soldiers. Soon, Otho, who had expected that adoption himself, was made emperor by the soldiers; both Galba and Piso were killed and Galba's head, having been cut off and fixed on a spear, was carried through the camp of the soldiers. Before he became emperor, many people had believed that Galba was most worthy of the emperorship; but after he had become emperor, they understood that they had been mistaken. Therefore, Galba was described by Tacitus in this way: 'capable of ruling had he not ruled.'

(a)   It was remarkable because there were four emperors in that year.
(b)   vītae pūblicae perītus erat = he was experienced in public life.
(c)   No. He was very mean and very strict.
(d)   No. He decided to take away a large part of the gifts which Nero had given to people, thus making many enemies.
(e)   No. He was well known to only a few people.
(f)   The soldiers would not have been thrilled because, on the adoption, they did not receive the customary largesse.
(g)   People thought, before Galba became emperor, that he would be most suitable to be emperor; but afterwards they realised that they had made a mistake.
(h)   Short, witty and very much to the point. It also happens to be poetic, since it scans as a hendecasyllable.

## Exercise 10.2

After Galba had been killed, Otho, who, although he had been a friend of Nero's, had already been made emperor by the soldiers, behaved himself better than was expected; but, before he became emperor, other soldiers had already decided to make Vitellius emperor. Otho announced in a letter that he would be willing to marry the daughter of Vitellius and share the emperorship with him; but a battle had already broken out between the supporters of Otho and those of Vitellius; the latter won. Then, because he greatly hated civil war, Otho refused to make (fight) another battle and committed suicide. The poet Martial wrote an epigram about this matter; having described Otho's hatred of civil war, he finished his epigram with these words: 'Let Cato, during his life, be greater admittedly even than Caesar; (but) in his death, was he in any way greater than Otho?'

## Exercise 10.3

Vitellius was famous for his gluttony; his meals cost the state a vast amount of money. He had a fat stomach and a face reddened by wine; he was not experienced in military matters. He was chosen by some soldiers but thrown down by others. Having tried to hide himself in Rome, he was recognised and most cruelly killed by citizens. His body was dragged into the river Tiber. After Vitellius, Titus Flavius Vespasianus was made emperor by the soldiers. Together with his son Titus, he was putting down most harshly the rebellion of the Jews who wished to be free. He